ENCHILADAS

AZTEC TO TEX-MEX

ENCHILADAS

AZTEC TO TEX-MEX

Cappy Lawton & Chris Waters Dunn

TRINITY UNIVERSITY PRESS
SAN ANTONIO, TEXAS

Published by Trinity University Press
San Antonio, Texas 78212

Book design by Andréa Caillouet

Portions of "Huitlacoche," "Mexican Oregano," "Epazote," "Cilantro," and "Mexican Mint Marigold" originally appeared in the *San Antonio Express-News*. Copyright © 2011. Used by permission.

Image credits: Andréa Caillouet, 6–7, 10, 11, 13, 16, 19, 41, 64. Chris Waters Dunn, xi, 86. Sunni Hammer, xiv, xvii, xxi, xxii–xxiii, 4, 8, 15, 20, 24, 27, 28, 30, 37, 38, 42, 46–47, 52, 56, 61, 62, 75, 78, 114, 126, 150, 188, 212, 226. Gabriel Ibarra, 23. Mark Menjivar, v, vi–vii, viii–ix, x, xii–xiii, xviii, xxiv, 33, 51, 76–77, 166.

Trinity University Press strives to produce its books using methods and materials in an environmentally sensitive manner. We favor working with manufacturers that practice sustainable management of all natural resources, produce paper using recycled stock, and manage forests with the best possible practices for people, biodiversity, and sustainability. The press is a member of the Green Press Initiative, a nonprofit program dedicated to supporting publishers in their efforts to reduce their impacts on endangered forests, climate change, and forest-dependent communities.

There are many inherent risks in the use of raw, prepared, and processed food ingredients during the cooking process. Additionally, some of the recipes in this book may include ingredients to which individuals may have a known or unknown allergy. Every effort has been made to present the best possible direction and advice with regard to the preparation of food recipes presented in this book. The publisher and authors assume no liability for any injury, allergic or other reaction, or damage incurred as a result of the information presented in this book.

The paper used in this publication meets the minimum requirements of the American National Standard for Information Sciences—Permanence of Paper for Printed Library Materials, ANSI 39.48–1992.

Printed in China

978-1-59534-751-0 HARDCOVER

978-1-59534-752-7 EBOOK

CIP DATA ON FILE AT THE LIBRARY OF CONGRESS

19 18 17 16 15 ǀ 5 4 3 2 1

Enchiladas del Suelo * PAGE 90

Enchiladas Verdes de Pollo * PAGE 146

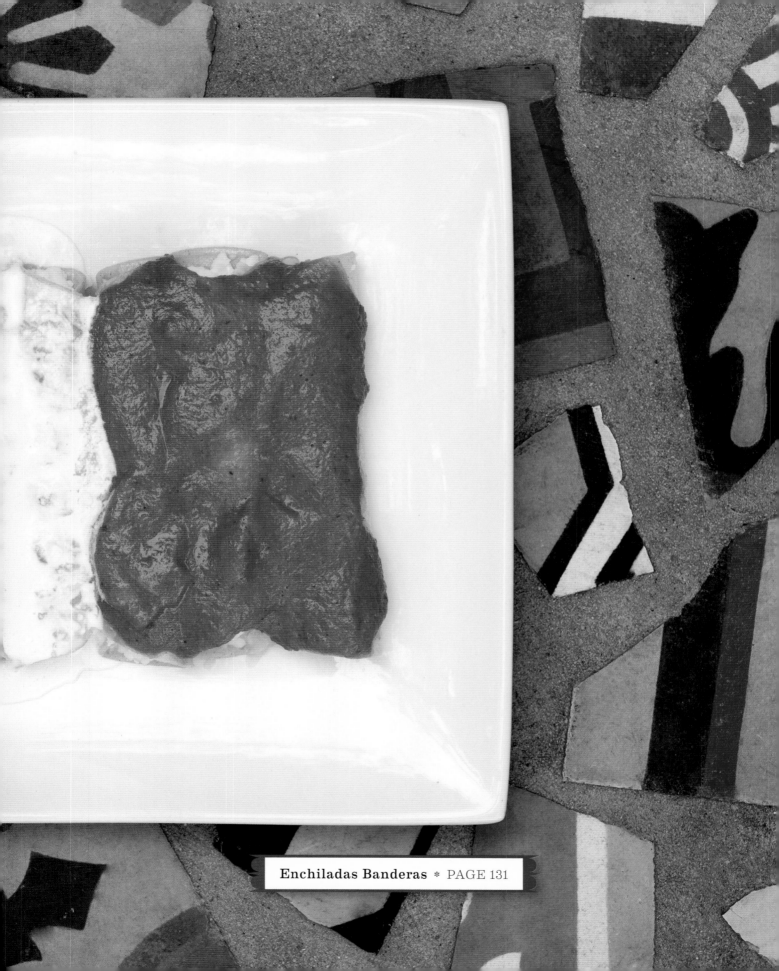

Enchiladas Banderas * PAGE 131

Enchiladas de Langosta * PAGE 164

Enchiladas de Camarón * PAGE 154

Enchiladas Callejeras * PAGE 148

Enchiladas Motuleñas * PAGE 112

Contents

Part 3: Recipes

Accompaniments / Guarniciones

Pork / Carne de Cerdo Enchiladas

Beef / Carne de Res Enchiladas

Enchiladas Potosinas * PAGE 98

Enchiladas Norteñas * PAGE 118

Enchiladas de Camote * PAGE 198

Pipián and Pork Enchiladas * PAGE 97

Mexico: A Culture of Corn and Enchiladas

In Mexico, the word *enchilada* isn't just for food. When a woman gets angry, it is said she becomes "enchilada"; to say that something is difficult to do, one would say, "no son enchiladas" ("they aren't [as easy as making] enchiladas"); to request more of something, one would say "enchilame otra." These examples demonstrate how important enchiladas are in the everyday life of the people of Mexico. Perhaps it is because enchiladas and Mexicans share a common history and culture—a history and culture that began with corn.

Journalist Michael Pollan aptly describes corn as a "miraculous grass."[1] It is nothing short of miraculous that this descendant of an ancient grass exists at all, considering it was developed by the convergence of three factors: nature, human-kind, and chance. The consequences of that convergence are equally remarkable. No other plant has had a greater impact on human life than corn.

Today, corn is the most produced grain in the world, cultivated on every continent except Antarctica.[2] This is because corn is an exceptionally adaptable and efficient engine of food production, capable of generating more food with less light, water, and nutrients than most other plants.[3]

The economic result is that corn, for good and bad, now appears in more food and food-related products than any other ingredient except salt. In recent decades it has even found its way into fuel, plastics, packaging, adhesives, chemicals, and pharmaceuticals. But none of this happened overnight.

According to P.J. White and L.A. Johnson in *Corn: Chemistry and Technology,* corn most likely was derived from wild grasses native to Central Mexico called "teosinte" that were cultivated by the Olmec and Mayan peoples. The earliest archaeological evidence of this dates from 7000 BCE from a cave in Mexico's valley of Tehuacán. By that time, White and Johnson say it "already had been hybridized to the point of no longer being able to reproduce without human assistance."

Reciprocally, the civilizations that evolved in Central America became dependent on corn for their own existence. The capital of the Aztec nation, Tenochtitlán (located where Mexico City is today), is estimated to have had a population of over 200,000, making it one of the most populous cities on earth before the Spanish Conquest of 1519–1521.[4] And it was corn that made such a large population possible.

To the people of Mexico, corn was both a literal and a spiritual source of life. It was worshipped in the form of several deities, both male and female. According to the sacred book of the Maya, *Popol Vuh,* man and woman were fashioned out of corn.

Today, corn is still revered by the Mexican people and remains an essential part of their diet. Perhaps their special relationship with this grain is best illustrated by the Tortilla Riots in 2007, when Mexicans took to the streets protesting the rising cost of corn, chanting, "Sin maíz, no hay país" ("Without corn, there is no country").

Nixtamalization

During the many centuries Mesoamericans spent hybridizing corn, they discovered that when the grain was soaked in a heated alkaline solution of slaked lime (calcium hydroxide), a process called "nixtamalization," the grain became easier to grind and tasted better. The nutritional content also increased and mycotoxins (fungal toxins) in the corn decreased. Once the nixtamalized corn was ground, patted into a flat, round shape, and baked on a clay *comal* (griddle), it became the staff of life for the Mexican people—the tortilla—which in turn made the enchilada possible.

The Tortilla

Most cultures on earth have some form of flatbread, from the chapati of India to the yufka of Turkey and the flatbrød of Norway. Mexico's flatbread, the tortilla, became the primary source of nutrition for its indigenous people and, in some instances, the only food they had. *El Códice Mendoza,* written about twenty years after the Spanish Conquest, describes Aztec children living on half a tortilla a day until three years of age, one whole tortilla from ages four to five, a tortilla and a half from ages six to twelve, and after thirteen years of age when they were expected to do adult work, two tortillas per day.[5]

Despite the harsh lives of most of the native population, especially under Spanish rule, the people survived. Fortunately, corn tortillas contain many of the nutritional attributes of a modern health food—they are naturally high in calcium and fiber, low in sodium, contain no cholesterol, and are gluten-free. (Note that the recipes in this book are gluten-free, with the exception of the Tex-Mex enchiladas made with ancho chile gravy.)

Tortillas are easy to make but difficult to make well. The simplicity of the ingredients—nixtamalized corn and water—is the reason for their complexity. It takes great skill to "feel" when the dough has just the right moisture content, is malleable but not too soft, thin enough to be tender without falling apart, and thick enough to be substantial but not so thick as to be tough. Traditionally, a good tortilla was considered so essential in Mexican culture that a young woman was deemed ready for marriage when she could make a good one.

With the advent of the tortilla, the invention of the enchilada was inevitable. After all, in a society where people ate with their hands, what better way to enjoy mole, salsa, beans, or other fillings than with a rolled or folded tortilla?

The Enchilada

The origin of the enchilada predates written history, but the word *enchilada* is more recent, first appearing in print during the 19th century.[6] *Enchilada* translates as "to season with chile," or one could say "to chilify" something. For this book, the definition of an enchilada is a corn tortilla, never flour, that is rolled, folded over or flat, filled or unfilled, and sauced (in a few instances, the sauce is incorporated into the dough).

Spanish Franciscan friar and chronicler Bernardino de Sahagún, in his 16th-century *Historia general de las cosas de Nueva España*, gives an eyewitness account of vendors at a market selling tortillas "enrolladas hechas redondas" (coiled up or rolled around) various fillings. He describes them in great detail: some were yellow, some were white, some were stuffed with mashed beans or with meat and ground chiles, others were "smeared" with a chile sauce, and some were "doubled over or folded."[7]

Recipes similar to the enchiladas Sahagún described are still made in Mexico today, along with many other versions that evolved over the subsequent centuries. As the culture and politics changed and evolved in Mexico, so did the enchilada.

Common pre-Columbian fillings were probably beans, squash, seeds, chiles, bird or turtle eggs, and small amounts of wild game or seafood.

During the Colonial period of the 16th–18th centuries, indigenous ingredients were augmented or replaced with cheese, pork, chicken, and other Spanish-influenced ingredients. And when France invaded Mexico in the mid-19th century, many French culinary influences were incorporated.

The latter 19th century and beginning of the 20th century saw a renewed appreciation for enchiladas made from what Mexicans deemed "traditional" recipes. Local versions of enchiladas, tamales, and tacos became associated with pride of country and patriotism.

Neighbors to the north, particularly in Texas and New Mexico, gave enchiladas their own unique interpretations by mixing elements of Mexican, European, cowboy, and Native American cultures.

Today, diners encounter enchiladas that reflect the entire history of Mexico, from pre-Columbian papadzules and simple bean and tortilla enfrijoladas to traditional favorites, such as enchiladas de mole and enchiladas verdes, as well as modern versions that defy categorization.

Taken as a whole, these recipes reflect the political, religious, and social influences that shaped Mexican culture through the ingredients that were used throughout its history. The enchilada is not only a delicious everyday Mexican food but a historic dish that embodies thousands of years of Mexican life.

Pipián Sauce * PAGE 96

How to Use This Book

The variations on enchilada recipes are seemingly endless, but the basic methods for preparing many ingredients are often the same, such as dry roasting or fire roasting chiles, making and using tortillas, preparing fillings made from beans, chicken, and pork, and the process of assembly. Once these fundamentals are mastered, the preparation of many recipes becomes familiar and easy.

These methods are presented in detail in Part 2: Fundamentals. It is highly recommended that this section be read before attempting the recipes in order to gain a greater understanding of how tortillas, fillings, and sauces are made. Page references for these topics are also provided within the recipes.

Some topics covered are:

* How to make tortillas
* Store-bought tortillas
* Fire roasting fresh chiles
* Dried chile preparation
* Dry roasting tomatoes, onions, garlic, and fresh chiles
* How to prepare dried beans and refried beans
* How to prepare Mexican rice
* How to prepare chicken, pork, beef, and other meats for fillings
* How to assemble enchiladas, including softening tortillas, filling, rolling, and saucing
* Tips on garnishing

Part 1: Ingredients offers helpful information regarding other key ingredients including avocados, tomatoes, tomatillos, and nopales, as well as information on Mexican herbs and spices, salt, and using lard versus vegetable oil.

There is also a section that provides an alphabetical list of Mexican cheeses commonly used with enchiladas. It describes their flavor profiles, textures, melting properties, and possible substitutes that can be used when a specific Mexican cheese is not available.

The most common fresh and dried chiles used in enchilada cookery are presented with a general description of their flavor profiles, from lowest to highest heat levels, and their uses.

A glossary is provided to assist with translation of Spanish words and terms used in this book.

PART 1:
Ingredients

Chiles

Chiles are the fruit of the genus *Capsicum,* in the nightshade family *Solanaceae,* which includes tomatoes, potatoes, eggplants, and tobacco. Capsicums originated in South America, but through nature and trade, spread outward. Chile seeds have been found at archeological sites in Tehuacán Valley, Mexico, that indicate people there were eating chiles 9,000 years ago.[1] By the time Europeans arrived in the Americas, chiles were an integral part of pre-Columbian society, used for medicine, tribute, weaponry, and especially as an ingredient in food.

During the 16th century, Portuguese and Spanish traders introduced chiles to most of Europe, the Middle East, Africa, and Asia, and this revolutionized many world cuisines. Korean kimchi, Thai and Indian curries, Hungarian goulash, and Spanish paella are just a few examples of chiles' almost universal popularity. What attracts humans to chiles is their heat, prompting a never-ending quest for the perfect balance between too much or too little of it.

The key ingredients that deliver all this fire and fervor are capsaicinoids, and in particular, capsaicin—an odorless, colorless compound that in nature protects the fruit from depredation by mammals and fungi. Interestingly, birds are immune to its irritating effect and are the principal means of spreading chile seeds in nature. Several species of chiles are commonly referred to as "bird chiles."

Most of the capsaicin is concentrated in the membranes attached to the inner walls of the fruit, and removing them will reduce the spiciness. Contrary to common belief, the seeds themselves do not contain much capsaicin, so removing them doesn't significantly change the heat level. In Mexican cuisine, seeds of dried chiles are usually removed when making moles or sauces (the seeds are often saved for other uses), but when using small, fresh chiles, such as jalapeños, serranos, and habaneros, the seeds are usually not removed.

The heat varies greatly even within the same variety. For example, one jalapeño can be relatively mild and another fiery hot. So it's a good idea to taste chiles before adding them to a recipe.

When someone accidentally overdoses on capsaicin, drinking water or beer actually makes matters worse, because capsaicin tends to repel water—much like pouring water on a grease fire. In the United States, milk is recommended as an antidote, but in Mexico salt is the most popular remedy. (In fact, salt plays a key role in moderating the spiciness of chiles in Mexican food recipes.)

Also, because chiles can burn the skin as well as the mouth, food preparation gloves are highly recommended when processing large amounts of chiles or when working with the more potent varieties such as habaneros. If a chile does burn the skin, a cut tomato pressed against the irritation will help. Some cooks wash their hands in water mixed with a little bleach to disperse the chile oils.

Chiles are easy to grow, especially in warmer and more humid climates, and can be quite prolific—usually a few plants will provide all the fire a family needs. If starting from seed, plant indoors or in a greenhouse 8–10 weeks before the last frost. When transplanting chiles to a garden, it is best to keep different species separated, because many varieties crossbreed easily.

It should be noted, however, there is no way to duplicate the terroir of the microclimates in Mexico or the unique flavor characteristics of the chiles grown there. For example, the chile chilhuacle, chile chilcostle, and chile pasilla oaxaqueña are essential ingredients for certain traditional moles and are not grown outside of their native Oaxaca. Even in the United States, the Anaheim chile of California is quite different in flavor from the nearly identical species grown in New Mexico.

The many subvarieties, differences in terroir, and regional variations of names for the same chile can make learning about them challenging. Even the word *chile* may be spelled "chilli," "chile," or "chili," depending on geographic locale. "Chile" is used in this book because it is the common spelling used in Mexico today, which is a Spanish translation of the original Nahuatl word *chilli*. In the United States, it is often spelled "chili," but it can also be an abbreviation for the dish chili con carne. The British spelling is "chilli" or "chilli pepper." (When Columbus landed in the Americas in 1492, he mistook the spiciness of chiles for black pepper (*Piper nigrum*), a totally unrelated species, which is why many people still mistakenly refer to chiles as "peppers.")

In spite of the complexities, it isn't difficult to gain a good working knowledge of commonly used chiles by learning to recognize them by appearance and flavor. Familiarity with the Capsicum family will yield the most amount of pleasure from chiles with the least amount of pain.

Fresh Chiles Commonly Used for Enchiladas

There's a degree of subjectivity in describing the flavor characteristics of different chiles as well as their heat levels. What follows is intended as a general description of chiles often used in enchilada recipes. However, every cook should develop his or her own personal "chile palate."

Poblano ✳ The poblano is one of the most widely used chiles in Mexican cuisine. It is large, 4–6 inches (10–15 cm) in length and 2–3 inches (5–8 cm) in diameter, with broad shoulders tapering to a point. The color is a dark green that turns deep red when ripe. The poblano is not used raw. Fire roasting deepens the flavor and facilitates removing the somewhat tough, waxy skin. Because of its shape and thick flesh, it is popular for chile rellenos (stuffed chiles). It can also be cut into *rajas,* or strips, and is often used puréed in sauces. The flavor is generally mild but occasionally can be fairly hot, so the heat level should be checked by tasting a small piece before using. The ancho is a dried version of the poblano, as is the darker mulato.

Jalapeño ✳ The jalapeño is probably the most easily recognized and widely consumed hot chile in the United States. It is 2–3 inches (5–8 cm) in length and about 1 inch (2 cm) in diameter with a rounded end, though size varies greatly. The flavor is reminiscent of the green vegetable notes in a bell pepper, and the heat ranges from relatively mild to medium hot. The color varies from medium green to dark green, and when mature, the fruit turns red and has a sweeter, hotter flavor. The jalapeño is used in everything from stews to guacamole, as a garnish for tacos and enchiladas, and stuffed as an appetizer. It is also popular pickled (*escabeche*).

Serrano ✴ This widely available chile is smaller in diameter, more bullet-like in shape, and much hotter than the jalapeño. The name refers to the mountains, or "sierras," in the states of Puebla and Hidalgo where it originated. It has a clean, white-hot heat and crisp acidity. It is used in fresh salsas, guacamole, sauces, and pickled.

Habanero ✴ The habanero is the hottest chile grown in Mexico and one of the most fruity and flavorful. Closely related to the Scotch bonnet and Jamaican Hot of the Caribbean, the habanero lends itself to fruity salsas, seafood marinades, and bottled sauces, and is essential to dishes from the Yucatán. The plant is beautiful and decorative, with dark green leaves and lantern-shaped fruit that can vary in size from 1 to 1 1/2 inches (2 to 4 cm) and in color from green to bright orange and red. Gloves should be worn when handling the fruit. The heat can be tamed somewhat by roasting and carefully removing the membranes inside.

Dried Chiles Commonly Used for Enchiladas

Ancho ✴ Ancho means "wide" in Spanish, which is a good description of both the shape of the chile and its broad popularity in Mexican cuisine. It is a dried version of the poblano. (Fresh and dried versions of the same chile often have different names.) The ancho can be distinguished from its darker relative, the mulato, by its orange-red color when a piece is held up to the light. It is wrinkly, 4–5 inches (10–13 cm) long, and approximately 3 inches (8 cm) in width. Try to choose anchos that are flexible and fragrant, which indicates freshness. Mild to medium-hot, it has an earthy flavor that is fruity and sweet with notes of coffee, raisins, and plums.

Mulato ✴ The mulato, like the ancho, is a dried poblano, but its color is a deep, dark brown, and it also exhibits a brown color when a piece is held up to the light. The flavor is also darker, with chocolate and licorice predominating and a heat level that is mild to medium-hot. When combined with the pasilla and the ancho, the mulato completes the "Holy Trinity" of chiles that are used to make many versions of moles.

Pasilla ✴ The true pasilla, also known as "chile negro," is the dried version of the chilaca chile. "True" is used here because in northern Mexico and in California the ancho, mulato, and poblano chiles are incorrectly called "pasilla." The true pasilla is easily recognized by its long, narrow shape, which is 5–6 inches (13–15 cm) long and 1–1 1/2 inches (2–4 cm) wide, and by its dark, raisin brown, almost black color. The flavor is herbaceous, with fruity tones of berry and raisin, and it is slightly sharper and hotter than the mulato or ancho. It is popular for use in seafood sauces as well as traditional moles.

Pasilla de Oaxaca ✴ The pasilla de Oaxaca, also known as "chile Mixe," is only grown in Oaxaca. It is 3–4 inches (8–10 cm) long and 1–1 1/2 inches (2–4 cm) wide. When it is mature, it is smoke dried. It is very hot, with a persistent heat, and carries flavor notes of smoke and tobacco.

Guajillo * The guajillo is a widely available, inexpensive, and popular chile. It is relatively long and slim, ranging in size from 4 to 6 inches (10 to 15 cm) long and 1 to 1½ inches (2 to 4 cm) at the shoulder. The guajillo is easily recognized by its relatively smooth, orange-red skin. It is called "cascabel" (rattle) in the north central part of Mexico and should not be confused with the little round chile of the same name. It is used to make sauces, as a purée to spread on meat, in stews, and is often mixed with anchos or other dried chiles. The flavor is sharp and tannic, and can vary from medium-hot to hot. Because the skin is tough, it is important to always strain guajillos that have been puréed.

Chile de Árbol * The name seems to indicate this chile comes from a tree (*árbol*), but it actually grows on a tall, woody bush. The chile averages about 3 inches (8 cm) in length and is very slender, about ¼ inch (⅔ cm) in width. It retains its bright red color when dried and is searingly hot. It is used in sauces, soups, and stews.

Chipotle Meco * Chipotles are mature red jalapeños that are smoked and dried. The word *chipotle* comes from the Nahuatl *chilpoctli*, meaning smoked chile. The meco variety, which comes from south and central Mexico, is approximately 2 inches (5 cm) long and about 1 inch (2 cm) wide, tan to medium tobacco-brown in color, and very wrinkled. The flavor is smoky, with notes of tobacco and chocolate. It has very deep, hot heat. Chipotles are used in stews, soups, and braising dishes.

Chipotle Morita * Morita is a smaller variety of chipotle, about 1–2 inches (2–5 cm) long and about ½ inch (1–1¼ cm) wide. It is from Chihuahua, where the majority of chipotles are grown in Mexico, and it is the most available chipotle in the United States. Because it is not smoked and dried for as long as the chipotle meco, it retains more of its reddish black color and some sweetness. It gets its name, "little mulberry or blackberry," because of its color. In the United States, morita chipotles will most likely be found preserved in adobo, a tomato-chile sauce, which gives the chile a dark reddish appearance. "Mora" chiles are a larger version of moritas.

Tomatoes and Tomatillos

In Spanish a tomato is called "tomate" or "jitomate."

The tomato, *Solanum lycopersicum,* is one of many culinary gifts Mexico gave the world, as important (or almost as important) as chocolate and vanilla. The plant originated in South America and is a member of the nightshade family along with potatoes and eggplants. The part we eat is technically a fruit—though most of us think of it as a vegetable.

In the northern part of Mexico, as well as in Spain, "tomate" refers to what people in the United States think of as a tomato, and "tomatillo" is the word used to describe another member of the nightshade family, *Physalis philadelphica.* This hard, green, tangy fruit visually resembles a small tomato and is easily recognizable by its papery husk.

In the central part of Mexico, however, the red tomato is referred to as "jitomate," which reflects its Nahuatl name *xitomatl,* and tomatillos are referred to as "tomate" or "tomate verde."

For this book, "tomato" and "tomatillo" will be used to differentiate between these red and green fruits.

How to Choose and Prepare Tomatoes

The Italian plum or Roma tomato is the best choice for an enchilada sauce because of its meaty texture and because it has fewer seeds than other varieties.

When using fresh tomatoes in salads or as a garnish, any flavorful, ripe, red tomato will do. For these applications, tomatoes are usually diced or sliced without removing the skins and seeds.

For other uses, some recipes call for blanching tomatoes in boiling water and then shocking them in ice water to facilitate removal of the skin. Other recipes call for blackening the tomatoes, using the same technique as for fire roasting chiles. Usually, the blackened skin is not discarded but included in the salsa.

How to Prepare Tomatillos

There are three basic ways to prepare tomatillos for use in an enchilada sauce.

Method 1: Fire roast the tomatillos (often with serranos or other small chiles) before blending.

Method 2: Blend raw ingredients and then fry the resulting sauce in a little oil.

Method 3: Boil ingredients together and then blend.

Where a particular method is traditional or preferred, it will be noted in the recipe.

Onions in Mexican Cuisine

Many of the recipes in this book call for white onions because they are the most commonly used bulb onion in Mexico. However, yellow onions can certainly be substituted if desired. In fact, many Mexican food restaurants in the United States exclusively use yellow onions for all their dishes simply because they are less expensive than other varieties. The flavor difference is subtle, but for absolute authenticity white is preferable.

Red onions, which have a more striking color and milder flavor than white or yellow onions, are popular for use raw in salads, uncooked salsas, and for garnishes, as well as in recipes that call for pickling.

When using any onion raw, the flavor is always improved by rinsing the diced or sliced onion with cold water and then blotting it dry with paper towels before adding it to a recipe. This helps reduce the amount of harsh sulfur compounds that are present in an uncooked onion—the same compounds that make some people tear up when chopping them.

Fresh Guacamole * PAGE 18

Avocados

The avocado originated in the state of Puebla in central Mexico, where the small, undomesticated variety "criollo," with its large seed and black skin, can still be found. Of the many hybrids that have been developed over the years, the Hass is the most popular and accounts for 80 percent of the avocados consumed in the world today. Its heritage can be traced back to a single seedling planted in the late 1920s by a mailman named Rudolph Hass in La Habra Heights, California.

Though avocados are most commonly appreciated for their buttery fruit, the leaves are also sometimes called for in Mexican cuisine, such as in the preparation of *frijoles negros* (black beans), in soups and stews, or as a bed for barbecuing meats. The flavor has been described as similar to a mixture of bay leaves and anise. These leaves come from a particular species of avocado grown in Mexico (*Persea drymifolia*) and are often available at Mexican specialty stores. Leaves from avocados commonly sold in the United States are not a good substitute.

One of the biggest challenges in dealing with avocados is accurately determining when they are ripe. The color of the skin isn't necessarily a reliable indicator of when an avocado is ready to eat—the best way to judge is by feel. Gently press the large rounded end (not the sides or stem end) of the fruit. When the avocado is ready for slicing, the rounded end will give slightly when pressed.

One or two more days ripening may be desirable when making guacamole, but there is a fine line between perfectly ripe and overripe. When in doubt, it is always better to choose a slightly firmer (not hard) avocado than a very soft one and to purchase an extra just in case. It is also a good idea to make sure the avocado has its stem intact and no apparent marks or indentations on the skin, which could indicate bruising.

An uncut avocado should not be refrigerated but can be stored in a wine refrigerator (set no lower than 55°F or 13°C), and it will keep nicely for several days. (This also works for tomatoes and bananas.)

Once cut, avocados are subject to enzymatic browning. In other words, when exposed to air, the flesh will quickly turn an unappetizing brown color. The best way to prevent this is to cut an avocado right before serving it. It also helps to sprinkle the surface of the flesh with lime or lemon juice, which not only inhibits browning but also brightens and balances the avocado's richness. Commercially available anti-browning agents are also effective.

If guacamole must be prepared ahead of time, sprinkle it with lime juice or a thin film of olive oil, press plastic wrap directly against the surface, and refrigerate. (The old wives' tale of imbedding the avocado seed in the guacamole to help preserve its color is a good story but doesn't really seem to do anything.)

How to Make Fresh Guacamole

Yields 2–3 cups (473–710 ml)

Ingredients:

* 3 tablespoons (27 grams) white onion, small dice
* 1 or more serrano or jalapeño chiles, destemmed and finely minced
* Kosher salt to taste
* 2 large avocados, skins and seeds removed, large dice
* Lime juice to taste
* 1 small unpeeled tomato, cored and deseeded, small dice
* 2 rounded tablespoons cilantro leaves, or to taste (optional)
* 1 tablespoon onion, small dice (optional)
* 1 tablespoon tomato, small dice (optional)
* 1 tablespoon cilantro, chopped (optional)

Directions:

* Place the diced onion and some of the minced chile in a molcajete (traditional Mexican grinding tool), sprinkle with a little salt, and mash to a pulp.
* Add the avocado, sprinkle with some lime juice, and continue mashing to a relatively smooth consistency (some texture is desirable).
* Stir in the diced tomato and cilantro.
* Taste and adjust the seasoning by adding more salt, lime juice, and/or a little more minced chile.
* Garnish with onion, tomato, and cilantro (optional).

Notes: Guacamole can also be prepared in a large bowl using the back of a fork or a potato masher. Don't worry about mashing the onion and chile—they will lend texture to the finished guacamole.

There are many other flavors that may be added to guacamole. Try using a mixture of citrus juices; stir in some chopped mandarin orange segments; or add a dash of olive oil.

Tips on Slicing Avocados

The best way to cut an avocado is to hold it lengthwise in the palm. Place the knife edge parallel to the avocado and cut into the side of the fruit. Without moving the blade, carefully rotate the avocado on the blade until it is cut all the way around. Gently twist the two avocado halves and pull apart. Set the halves on a cutting board, lightly whack the seed with the sharp edge of the knife, give it a half turn, and remove the seed. Holding thumb and forefinger on both sides of the spine (back) of the knife, carefully push the seed off the blade. (Never try to grab the seed from underneath the sharp side of a knife.) The avocado can then be peeled and sliced, or if is to be diced, the flesh can be crosscut in the skin and scooped out with a large spoon.

Nopales (Cactus Paddles)

Though the idea of eating a cactus may seem unusual to people in many parts of the world, it is a commonplace ingredient in Mexican cuisine. People there have eaten various species of cacti since pre-Columbian times, and the fruit and paddles continue to be one of the healthiest foods in their diet. A cup of boiled nopalitos contains only 22 calories and provides 2 grams protein, 3 grams fiber, and no fat.[1]

The word *nopales* comes from the Nahuatl word for cactus paddles, *nōpalli.* "Nopalitos" refers to cactus paddles that have been cut into strips or diced. The flavor is very mild, similar to the taste of cooked green beans. In Mexico, nopales are often served as a complement to a main dish but can also be the featured ingredient in salads, tacos, scrambled eggs, and enchiladas. Nopales flour is also sometimes used to make tortillas.

Freshly packaged nopalitos (raw, fresh nopales that are already cleaned and sliced) are available at many Mexican specialty stores. Avoid buying nopalitos if the edges are discolored. Nopalitos in jars or cans are usually brined and do not have the same flavor or quality as fresh.

When shopping for whole cactus paddles, look for firm, smooth ones that are about 6 inches (15 cm) in length and ¼ inch (6 mm) thick. To clean a paddle, hold it by the base with a gloved hand, and scrape off the thorns and surface bumps by cutting with a knife against the direction of the spines. Be careful not to cut away the entire outer layer of the nopal. When cleaned, the paddle can be cut into small squares or strips, or it can be scored and grilled whole.

How to Cook Nopales

Nopales release a viscous liquid similar to okra when cooked. Some people find it unappetizing, but rinsing the nopales helps remove a lot of it. Interestingly, the juice from the fruit of cacti is sold as a health food because it is high in fiber and betalains, a powerful antioxidant.

Method 1: Prepare raw (preferred method, especially for salad, see page 83)

Clean and cut the nopales into strips about the width of a green bean. Place the strips in a bowl and massage with a little kosher salt. Spread out on a sheet pan and refrigerate for an hour.

Rinse thoroughly and the strips are ready to use. This method will not remove as much of the viscous liquid as simmering or sautéing, but it preserves the fresh color and flavor of the cactus.

Method 2: Grill, dry roast on a comal or iron griddle, or sauté in a pan

The cactus paddles can be left whole, scored by making a few slashes on the surface of the paddle, or cut into "fingers" that remain attached at the base. Place on a hot grill, comal or griddle, or in a sauté pan, and turn as the paddles begin to change color. Continue cooking until they are tender and almost cooked through.

Method 3: Simmer

Yields about 6 cups (1.4 liters)

Ingredients:

* 2 pounds (907 grams) nopales, cleaned and cut into strips
* 1 small white onion, peeled and quartered
* 1 small bunch cilantro, tied together with butcher's twine
* Kosher salt to taste

Directions:

* Place the prepared nopalitos, onion, and cilantro in a large saucepan.
* Cover with water by about 1 inch.
* Bring the water to a boil and add salt to taste.
* Cook until the nopalitos are tender but not overly soft, 8–10 minutes.
* Remove and discard the onion and cilantro.
* Drain the nopalitos and lightly rinse to remove the viscous liquid.
* Blot with paper towels to dry.
* Taste and adjust the seasoning.

Note: *May be covered and refrigerated for 1–2 days.*

Huitlacoche (Corn Fungus)

Huitlacoche, or cuitlacoche, is actually a fungus that grows on corn plants causing the kernels to swell, turn white, and become filled with a thick black substance that is the secret to huitlacoche's success. The fungus only appears under the right conditions—during intervals of warm, wet weather. But when it does, it increases the dollar value of an ear of corn by as much as twenty to fifty times. Therefore, farmers in Mexico, like their Aztec ancestors, consider huitlacoche a gift from the gods and pray for its arrival.

American corn farmers, on the other hand, pray (and spray) to prevent huitlacoche from appearing. In fact, they refer to it by an entirely different name—"corn smut." Perhaps this is why so many euphemistic names such as "Mexican caviar" and "Mexican truffle" have been given to huitlacoche in order to counter its less savory monikers; but by whatever name it's called, the flavor is creamy, earthy, and slightly sweet, with woodsy, mushroom overtones. It is a true delicacy when used as a filling for quesadillas, empanadas, tacos, tarts, and enchiladas.

How to Prepare Huitlacoche

Yields approximately 1 pound (454 grams)

Ingredients:

* 1 tablespoon (15 grams) vegetable oil or lard
* 1 small white onion, peeled and diced
* 1 (14.8 ounce, 420 grams) can huitlacoche (see notes)
* Kosher salt to taste
* 1 tablespoon (1 gram) fresh epazote, chopped (optional)

Directions:

* Heat the oil or lard in a sauté pan over medium heat. Add the onion and cook, stirring occasionally, until they are translucent but not browned, 3–5 minutes.
* Add the huitlacoche and (optional) epazote and cook until the liquid is reduced.
* Add salt to taste.

Notes: *Huitlacoche is generally only available canned in the United States.*
Some chefs like to add sautéed button mushrooms to the huitlacoche.

Mexican Chorizo

Mexican chorizo is quite different from the Spanish sausage of the same name. Spanish chorizo is usually a firm, cured sausage that gets its deep red color from a generous addition of smoky paprika. Spanish chorizo can be sliced and eaten uncooked or used as an ingredient in many dishes. Mexican chorizo is sold fresh and must be cooked before eating. It gets its color from the addition of chiles and *achiote* (annatto seed) and is removed from its casing (if it has one) before cooking. Because there is no need to stuff the sausage into casings, it's easy to make at home.

How to Make Chorizo

Yields 6.5 pounds (2.95 kilos)

Ingredients:

* 10 guajillo chiles (60 grams), destemmed, deseeded, and dry roasted (see page 58)
* 1 ½ cups (335 ml) apple cider vinegar, warmed
* 3 cloves garlic, peeled
* 2 tablespoons (1.5 grams) fresh marjoram, finely chopped
* 2 teaspoons (1 gram) dried Mexican oregano or 2 tablespoons (1.75 grams) fresh Italian oregano, finely chopped
* 2 tablespoons (56 grams) achiote (annatto) paste
* 3 tablespoons (27 grams) kosher salt, or to taste
* 1 rounded tablespoon (7 grams) freshly ground black pepper
* 5 pounds (2.25 kilos) ground pork

Directions:

* Place the prepared chiles in a blender.
* Add vinegar, 1 cup (237 ml) water, garlic, marjoram, oregano, achiote, salt, and black pepper and process until smooth.
* Place the pork in a large bowl.
* Add the blended ingredients to the pork and mix well (use clean, gloved hands).
* Test the mixture by frying 1 tablespoon of sausage in a sauté pan. Taste and adjust the seasoning.
* For the best flavor, cover and refrigerate overnight before using.

Note: *Chorizo may be covered and stored in a refrigerator for up to 5 days or in a freezer for up to 1 month.*

Cecina (Mexican Salted Dried Beef)

In Mexico, cecina is thinly sliced meat that has been salted and hung to dry in the sun. Before the advent of refrigeration, this was an important and necessary means of preserving food. This curing process continues today, but it is done instead to achieve the resulting flavor and texture. Cecina, prosciutto, bresaola, and beef jerky are all examples of the magic that salt, air, and time can perform on meat.

Cecina is usually made from a less fatty cut of beef such as rump, brisket, or flank that is cut with, not against, the grain. Yecapixtla, in the state of Morelos, is famous for its expert "cecineros," who can slice large cuts of beef into paper thin pieces of meat several yards long, which are easier to handle when placing outdoors to dry.

How to Make Cecina

Yields 1.5 pounds (680 grams)

Ingredients:

* 1 piece of beef rump, brisket, or flank, trimmed of fat and cut into a rectangle about 12 inches (30 cm) long (running with the grain), 4–5 inches (10–13 cm) wide, and 2–3 inches (5–8 cm) thick
* Kosher salt
* Lime juice
* Black pepper (optional)

Directions:

* Starting at a narrow end and slicing with the grain, cut a ¼-inch (6 mm) piece down the length of the meat, stopping about ¼ inch (6 mm) from the end. Rotate the meat 180 degrees and repeat, again stopping just before reaching the end.
* Continue rotating and cutting to produce even slices that are hinged together like a folding door.
* If desired, gently unfold and pound the meat to make it even thinner.
* Generously sprinkle both sides of the unfolded meat with salt.
* Refold the meat, place on a rack set over a plate, and refrigerate for 8–12 hours.
* Hang unfolded meat over a wooden dowel and place in the sun approximately 2–4 hours, or until the meat is dry but not stiff.
* Sprinkle with lime juice and (optional) black pepper and move to a shady spot. Allow the meat to hang 2–3 more days, until completely dry. (Drape cheesecloth over it to discourage insects, and bring indoors at night to avoid dampness.)
* To cook cecina, it should be lightly oiled and placed on a grill or under a broiler for just a couple of minutes on each side. Overcooking will make it tough.

Notes: Partially frozen meat and a very sharp granton carving knife are the perfect tools for the job.

Cecina should not be confused with Cecina Enchilada, which is a thinly pounded pork cutlet that is marinated in a paste of chiles and spices and then cooked.

Enchiladas Huastecas con Huevos * PAGE 168

Crema Mexicana (Mexican Cultured Cream)

When sour cream is called for in a Mexican recipe, it is usually a substitute for crema Mexicana, which is more like crème fraiche or cultured cream, rather than the sour cream commonly sold in the United States.

In the United States, sour cream is made from cultured cream with approximately 20 percent butterfat, along with additional ingredients, such as carrageenan and guar gum. It is usually thicker and sourer than French crème fraiche and crema Mexicana, which are made from cultured cream with a higher fat content (as high as 30 percent). The higher butterfat content makes crème fraiche and crema Mexicana richer tasting than sour cream and more resistant to curdling when heated.

If unavailable, crema Mexicana can easily be made at home.

How to Make Crema Mexicana

Yields 1 cup (237 ml)

Ingredients:

* 1 cup (237 ml) whipping cream
* 1 tablespoon (15 ml) buttermilk

Directions:

* To sterilize a tempered glass container, fill it with water, place it in a microwave, and heat to a boil. Carefully pour out the water and set the container aside to cool for a few minutes.

* When the container has cooled, pour in the whipping cream, add the buttermilk, and gently swirl to mix.

* Cover with plastic wrap and set aside at room temperature 12–18 hours, or until the cream has thickened.

* Stir, re-cover, and refrigerate until needed. It will continue to thicken and will keep refrigerated for about 1 week.

__Note:__ If a recipe calls for jocoque, it usually means a product similar to Greek style yogurt, also called "labneh" in the Middle East. It was introduced to Mexico by Lebanese immigrants and is sometimes used as a substitute for crema Mexicana. In the area of Mexico where Michoacán and Jalisco meet, crema Mexicana is called "jocoque."[1]

Mexican Cheeses

It's hard to imagine enchiladas without cheese, but the pre-Columbian people of Mexico did not eat dairy products. Milk and cheese, along with cows and goats, arrived with the Spanish conquistadors. Once cheese was introduced, however, it soon became an important ingredient of Mexican cuisine. A food high in protein, fat, and salt—all of which were hard to come by in 16th-century Mexico—would assuredly have been held in high esteem.

By the end of the Colonial period (1650–1810), cheese had become a staple in the Mexican kitchen. It was during this time that Mexico's unique types of cheese were developed, often inspired by European counterparts but influenced by local and regional tastes, climate, and cuisine. Many of these cheeses are still produced in homes or as a cottage industry, but some especially popular types such as queso fresco and Oaxaca are manufactured nationally on an industrial scale.

Most Mexican cheeses are made from raw cows' milk, some are made from raw goats' milk, and some are made using a combination of both. The widespread use of unpasteurized milk in Mexican cheeses prohibits many of them from being legally imported into the United States because of the danger of bacterial contamination. Of particular concern are fresh cheeses that aren't aged long enough to kill harmful pathogens present in raw milk. Luckily, pasteurized versions of many of the most popular Mexican cheeses, such as queso fresco, panela, and Oaxaca, are now being produced north of the border and are widely available. They do not reflect the terroir of the originals, but they are good alternatives especially when fresh cheese is called for in a recipe.

Popular Mexican Cheeses for Enchiladas

Adobera * *A mild cows' milk cheese that gets its name from its adobe brick shape*

It has a soft, breakable texture. It softens when heated and is typically used in enchiladas. If unavailable, any other mild cheese such as asadero or Monterey Jack may be substituted.

Asadero * *A white, semisoft, mild cows' milk cheese that melts well*

It is a version of Oaxaca cheese that is pressed into a brick shape. It is sometimes marketed as queso quesadilla. Asadero is used for queso fundido, rellenos, and quesadillas. Provolone, fontina, teleme, Monterey Jack, and Muenster are widely available substitutes.

Chihuahua * *A semihard cheese named for the state of its origin*

It is sometimes called queso Menonita because it was first made by Mennonite immigrants who came to Mexico from Canada in the early 20th century. The original version has small holes and is reminiscent of white English Cheshire cheese. The color is pale yellow to white; taste varies from sharp to mild. White cheddar or Monterey Jack are good alternatives.

Cotija * *A firm cows' milk cheese named for the city of the same name in Michoacán*

It is one of only two Mexican cheeses protected by law (the other is queso de bola of Ocosingo, Chiapas). Cotija must be made of pasteurized milk. Because of its hard, crumbly texture and salty flavor, it is usually grated over food as an accent. Cotija de Montaña is seasonally produced from July to October using only milk from grassfed cows and is somewhat similar to Parmesan; Tajo is a cotija cheese that is more moist and similar in texture to Greek feta. Parmesan or Greek mizithra are good substitutes for cotija.

Mexican Manchego * *A semihard cows' milk or cows' and goats' milk cheese*

It was inspired by the Spanish version but is quite different. It is rindless, buttery, and melts well. Manchego Viejo is a firm, aged version. Monterey Jack is a good substitute.

Oaxaca * *A semisoft, mild cows' milk cheese named for the state where it was created*

This popular cheese is now made nationally. The process of stretching and rolling the curd into a ball creates a stringy texture reminiscent of mozzarella. Because of its melting properties, it is often used for quesadillas. Mozzarella is a good substitute.

Panela * *An unaged skim milk cheese, soft but slightly chewy*

It is traditionally sold in baskets and called "queso de canasta." When grilled or browned, it softens but doesn't melt. The way panela reacts to heat is reminiscent of Indian Paneer or Cypriot halloumi, which are good substitutes.

Queso Añejo * *A relatively young aged version of queso fresco, similar to feta*

As queso añejo continues to age, it becomes a firm cheese similar to Parmesan, Romano, or even an aged Gouda. It is traditionally made from goats' milk but is more commonly available made with cows' milk. It is good for baking, stuffing enchiladas, grilling, or garnishing. It is often sold "enchilado" or coated with dried and ground paprika or other mild chile. A good substitute for queso añejo is queso fresco that has been placed in a strainer lined with cheesecloth and set over a bowl in the refrigerator. Let the cheese dry for a week before using.

Queso Blanco * *Also called queso sierra or queso enchilada*

An unaged skim cows' milk cheese that is a pressed version of queso fresco. It has a soft texture and often has a citrus flavor note when lime juice is used for the coagulant. It softens but does not melt when heated.

Queso Fresco   ✳   *As the name implies, a fresh (unaged) cheese*

Fresh cheeses are the most popular cheeses in Mexico, queso fresco being the most common. Its light, mild flavor balances well with spicy foods. It is made with whole cows' milk or a combination of cows' and goats' milk. It is not a melting cheese. The texture is somewhat spongy and crumbly and becomes rubbery when heated, so it is primarily used as a garnishing cheese to sprinkle over the top of dishes (though it often finds its way into a chile relleno or enchilada filling). Like any fresh cheese, it has a short shelf life. A mild feta can be substituted for it. It can also be easily made at home (see page 34).

Requesón   ✳   *A very soft whole cows' milk cheese*

Requesón is often sold at markets wrapped in corn husks. It is somewhat similar to a very lightly salted mild ricotta or small curd cottage cheese in texture, and is used in enchiladas, cakes, tostadas, and cheese spreads. If substituting ricotta, try to use a less salty version.

Homemade Queso Fresco

All cheese is produced by coagulating the casein protein in milk and separating it, along with the milk fat, from the remaining watery liquid, called whey. This is achieved by heating and acidifying milk with lemon juice, lime juice, or vinegar, or by heating and acidifying milk and then adding rennet, a coagulant enzyme.

Queso fresco, meaning "fresh cheese," can be produced by simply warming and acidifying milk, which makes it one of the easiest cheeses to make. Panela, asadero, queso blanco, and Oaxaca cheeses are also made using this method. The individual characteristics of a cheese are determined by the way the curd is treated after it is separated from the whey.

Lime juice is a popular acidifier for making queso fresco in Mexico, particularly at home, but Luis Morales, graduate of the Culinary Institute of America Latin Cuisines Certificate Program and a professional cheese maker, recommends cider vinegar, because it has about twice the acidity as lime juice (making it a stronger coagulant) and adds background flavor to the finished product.

Salt can be added at the beginning of the process or at the end. If added to the milk at the beginning, much more salt is needed because so much liquid drains away. If added at the end, after the curd is formed, the salt is added to taste.

Morales says that to make good cheese, "you need time, space, and the right equipment." He also stresses that it is very important to meticulously wash hands and disinfect equipment because dairy products are very susceptible to bacterial contamination.

How to Make Queso Fresco with Vinegar

Yields 1–1.5 pounds (454–680 grams)

Equipment:

* A heavy-bottomed nonreactive (stainless steel or enameled) stockpot
* A large strainer
* Finely woven cheesecloth
* A large bowl
* A calibrated, instant-read thermometer

Ingredients:

* 1 gallon (3 ¾ liters) whole milk, raw or pasteurized, but not ultra-pasteurized
* 6 tablespoons (54 grams) kosher salt if added to the milk before heating, or salt to taste if adding after curd is separated
* 4–6 tablespoons (59–88 ml) apple cider vinegar

Directions:

* Place the stockpot over medium-low heat and add milk.

* Add 6 tablespoons (54 grams) salt (or salt to taste at the end of the process).

* Heat the milk slowly, stirring frequently, until it reaches 185°F (85°C) on an instant-read thermometer. Do not boil.

* Line the strainer with a triple layer of cheesecloth and set over a large bowl.

* When the milk is the right temperature, remove it from heat, gently stir in a circular motion, and add 4 tablespoons (59 ml) apple cider vinegar.

* Allow the milk to sit for a few minutes until the curds separate from the whey (white clumps will float in a bluish semitransparent liquid). Add up to 2 more tablespoons (30 ml) vinegar as needed to get a good separation.

* Very gently pour the curds and whey through the cheesecloth-lined strainer set over a bowl. Let drain for a few minutes. (Save the whey—it can be used in bread making, added to soups, stews, cooked cereals, and fruit smoothies, or as a food supplement for pets.)

* If salt was not added at the beginning of the process, now is the time to salt the curd. Gently fold a teaspoon at a time into the curd, wait a few minutes, taste, and add more as needed. Be aggressive with the seasoning because some of the salt will drain.

* When most of the whey has drained, gather the edges of the cheesecloth around the curd and tie securely. Hang the ball of cheese from the faucet arm over the kitchen sink, or tie it around a large wooden spoon and suspend it over a deep bowl. Let the cheese continue to drain for 2 hours, or longer for a drier product.

* The queso fresco is now ready to eat. It can also be placed in a cheese mold or canasta (cheese basket), if desired. (Japanese rice molds work well for this.) It should be refrigerated as soon as the whey is drained and it will have approximately the same expiration date as the milk from which it was made.

How to Make Queso Fresco with Lime Juice

Follow the same procedure as above, substituting ½ cup (118 ml) lime juice for the vinegar. The curd will be more delicate than when made using vinegar and must be handled very gently. It is also best to salt the cheese after the curd has separated.

Salt and Mexican Cuisine

The Conquest of New Spain is a memoir of the invasion of Mexico by Spain in 1519–1521, written by Bernal Díaz del Castillo, one of the soldiers who was there. In the account, the author makes numerous references to the necessity of salt and the difficulty the Spaniards, and even some Native Americans, had in acquiring enough of it. Díaz lamented the fact that the conquistadors didn't even have enough salt to dress their wounds, and the Tlascalan caciques (chiefs) said their people were afraid to leave their villages to search for salt because they were so "beleaguered" by the Aztecs.[1]

Their plight is understandable. Salt is the one mineral humans crave, and with good reason—we can't live without it. But today, many health experts warn that we can't live with it—that is, with the excessive amounts of salt most of us consume. The key is balance—use enough salt for optimal flavor enhancement but not so much that it is unhealthy.

Finding that balance can be difficult, but one way to achieve it is by developing a sense for seasoning. This is extremely important when preparing Mexican food, where salt plays such a vital role in balancing the heat of chiles, which are so central to the cuisine.

Taste the food periodically throughout the cooking process. Focus on every aspect of the flavor and ask what further seasoning the dish needs (or doesn't need). Salt is not the only answer. Sometimes a splash of lime or a pinch of sugar will suffice. Or perhaps all that is needed is a little more time for the flavors to meld.

When using salt, make sure it is pure and without additives because the type of salt used will greatly affect the flavor of the food. Common table salt contains additives, such as calcium silicate to make it free-flowing, as well as iodide, a trace nutrient that is often added to table salt. These additives mask the clean flavor of pure salt and should be avoided.

This is why kosher salt is preferred by many chefs—it has no additives. It also has a coarser grain, which makes it easier to handle and more accurate to deliver to the food, and it has roughly one-third to one-half the amount of sodium by volume as the same amount of fine-grained table salt. Expensive sea salts and flavored salts are interesting to work with but primarily intended to be used as "finishing" salts, such as sprinkling fleur de sel on a grilled steak right before serving it.

Using good quality pure salt and tasting enchilada fillings and sauces thoughtfully and often during preparation will ensure that dinner guests won't be looking for the salt shaker. They won't need it.

Herbs and Spices

Mexican Oregano

Despite its name, Mexican oregano isn't really oregano. Even more confusing, it isn't one particular plant but several. Plants referred to as "Mexican oregano" can be related to mint, bee balm, verbena, even coleus, but they all share one thing in common—an aroma and flavor reminiscent of true oregano coupled with an assertiveness that can stand up to spicy, hot foods better than many other herbs.

Italian oregano (*Origanum x majoricum*) and the Mexican oregano (*Poliomintha longiflora*) are both in the *Lamiaceae*, or mint, family, but the aromatic and pleasantly sweet flavor of the Italian oregano is mild by comparison to the pungent, sharp, boldness of its Mexican relative, making the Italian oregano a better choice for a delicate tomato sauce and the latter for a spicy enchilada sauce.

Poliomintha longiflora is popular and widely available in South Texas. It is deer, insect, and drought resistant and displays a profusion of delicate lavender blossoms all summer long.

Bolner's Fiesta Spices markets a similar-tasting but totally different herb as "Mexican Oregano." Tom Bolner says, "The oregano we process from Mexico comes from the area around San Luis Potosí and is *Lippia graveolens*."

A close relative of lemon verbena, it is the most likely herb to be sold as *orégano* in Mexico; it grows four to six feet in height and has clusters of small, cream-colored flowers that bloom virtually year round in warm climates.

Mexican oreganos have been used in folk medicine as a topical antiseptic, as a mouthwash, and as a treatment for sore throats and colds.

In the kitchen, Mexican oreganos pair well with allspice, chiles, cumin, garlic, lime, tomatoes, beans, chorizo, and beef. Mexican oregano's resilient flavor is not only excellent in enchilada sauces but also in marinades and adobos. Many cooks prefer to use it in its dried form because drying makes the herb milder and sweeter.

Epazote

At first glance, epazote is an unlikely candidate for Mexican herb fame. A member of the Goosefoot family of plants, this tenacious, gangly native of southern Mexico and Central and South America looks and behaves like a weed. It grows to three or more feet in height with irregular branches, long serrated leaves, and clusters of tiny green flowers at the tips of the stems.

Opposite: avocado leaves (left), Mexican oregano (right)

The original name comes from the Nahautl Indian words *epatl,* meaning "skunk," and *tzotl,* meaning "sweat," which is a pretty good indication that epazote has a rather assertive aroma. Common English names for epazote—"skunkweed," "pigweed," and "wormseed"—also raise questions from a culinary point of view. Some people detect the odor of creosote, others turpentine, musk, or more happily, lemon. But one thing is certain: there is more to epazote than meets the eye—and the nose.

Thousands of years ago, Aztecs recognized the importance of epazote medicinally, as well as culinarily. Though ingesting large amounts of the seed oil can be toxic, small amounts of the plant can be used as a remedy for parasites and worms, as an analgesic, as a carminative, and for stomach ailments. It also repels insects and therefore protects the other plants in the garden.

In the kitchen, it lends an earthy, lemony background note to eggs, potatoes, squash, and tomatoes, pork and crab dishes, huitlachoche, soups, mole de olla and mole verde, and sopes. But epazote is most famous for what it adds to, and takes away from, beans. This is because epazote not only adds its unique flavor to legumes; it also reduces the unpleasant side effect that often goes with eating them—gas—which makes epazote food-friendly, people-friendly, and a "weed" worth keeping around.

Cilantro

Cilantro is the Mexican name (and the most commonly used name in the United States) for the leaves of the coriander plant. It is one of the most widely used herbs in the world. The leaves, roots, and seeds show up in the cuisines of Asia, Africa, the Middle East, Latin America, and even Scandinavia.

But in spite of its universality, cilantro evokes extreme reaction—people either love it or hate it. While some describe the herb as citrusy, earthy, and nutty, others say it tastes and smells like soap.

Food author and scientist Harold McGee explains why. It has to do with aldehydes that are present in the plant and the way people perceive them. Aldehydes are organic compounds made up of modified fatty substances that are often quite pungent. And the aldehydes in cilantro are very similar to or the same as those found in soap or in the body fluids exuded by the bug family of insects. Some people may be genetically hardwired to dislike the herb because of a subliminal perception of it as something that shouldn't be eaten.[1] However, repeated exposure may diminish this negative reaction.

Aside from its controversial taste, cilantro is rather delicate. Always use a sharp knife when chopping it to prevent bruising the tender leaves. And remember that heat dissipates the flavor, so the herb should be used raw or added at the very end of cooking.

How to Preserve Cilantro

Cut ½ inch (12 mm) off the ends of the stems with a sharp knife, place the stems in a glass with a couple of inches of water in it, cover loosely with a plastic bag, and refrigerate. It should stay fresh for more than a week.

Note: *Don't confuse cilantro with culantro (Eryngium foetidum). They are closely related, but culantro, which is popular in many Caribbean and Asian cuisines, has much larger saw-toothed leaves and a considerably stronger taste and aroma.*

Canela (Cinnamon)

Cinnamon could be called the Spice of Conquest—it was introduced to Spain by Moorish invaders during the 8th century and subsequently brought to the New World by Spanish conquistadors in the early 16th century.

In both instances, the invaders were eventually overthrown, but not before the spice had found a permanent home in the native cuisines. In Mexico, the people soon discovered that cinnamon, which they call "canela," was the perfect complement to chocolate, moles, picadillos, and myriad other savory and sweet dishes. In fact, "Mexican chocolate" usually implies chocolate with cinnamon. Today, Mexico is the largest single importer of true cinnamon in the world.

"True" is used here for good reason. The spice referred to as cinnamon in the United States is usually cassia, a close relative of canela, or true cinnamon, the spice used in Mexican cuisine.

Canela is native to the island country of Sri Lanka (formerly Ceylon), and has a more delicate aroma and a subtler and sweeter flavor than the more strongly flavored cassia, which is cultivated in China, Vietnam, India, and Indonesia. Though the spices are similar, they are by no means identical and generally should not be substituted for each other. For example, cassia might be excellent in a curry, but true cinnamon is more appropriate for a Mexican mole.

Luckily, cassia and true cinnamon are easy to tell apart. When sold whole, as *canela entera*, true cinnamon is light beige in color and comprised of several thin layers of tender, inner bark that have been rolled into long, relatively brittle "quills." These quills are soft enough to break easily or pulverize in a mortar or electric grinder. By contrast, the woody "sticks" of cassia are much harder, rolled like a scroll, and are reddish brown in color.

Mexican Mint Marigold

Mexican mint marigold, also known as "yerbaníz," "Texas tarragon," "pericón," and "hierba de las nubes" (cloud plant), is a versatile, anise-flavored perennial, native to the mountains of Mexico and Guatemala.

It grows as an upright, bushy shrub, two to three feet in height, with spear-shaped, finely serrated leaves about 1½ inches (4 cm) long and ¼ inch (6 mm) wide. It is drought, heat, and insect resistant and attracts beneficial insects to a garden. In the fall, when many other flowering plants have faded, it produces masses of small, bright yellow-orange blooms.

It was first documented by Europeans in the 16th century. Legend has it that the Aztecs used the ground leaves in a powder they blew into the faces of ritual victims to calm them before sacrifice. It is still used in Mexico today as a medicinal tea for upset stomachs, to calm nerves, and as a cure for everything from colds to hangovers.

The blooms, because of their rich color and fragrance, are popular in fresh flower arrangements and add beauty to mixed green salads. Dried, the blossoms may be added to potpourris and sachets.

The leaves are an excellent substitute in any recipe calling for French tarragon, an herb which is difficult to grow in hot climates. Mexican mint marigold adds a subtle anise flavor to salads, eggs, fish and shellfish dishes, and chicken. It is also useful in vinaigrettes and flavored oils, in savory desserts, and for making a soothing anise-flavored tea.

Hoja Santa

Hoja santa, which means "sacred leaf" in Spanish, is a popular herb in Mexican cuisine. The broad, heart-shaped, velvety leaves can grow to the size of a dinner plate (12 inches, 30 cm) or larger, and are often used as a wrapper for fish, meat, and tamales. The leaves are also torn or chopped and added to soups, stews, beans, and moles, such as the famous mole verde from Oaxaca.

The flavor is elusive to describe but impossible to forget, evoking comparisons to sassafras, licorice, anise, or black pepper. (In fact, the plant is in the same botanical family as black pepper, *Piper nigrum.*) The aroma is reminiscent of sassafras or root beer, which is why it is commonly called "the root beer plant" in the United States.

Hoja santa is native to Mesoamerica and grows well in warm climates. Some gardeners will say that it grows too well—if not grown in a container or confined area, it can quickly spread and take over an entire garden.

The plant thrives in moist, well-drained soil and, when the weather is really hot, benefits from a little afternoon shade. It will die back in freezing weather but will usually come back in the spring. It is an eye-catching ornamental plant and very useful in the Mexican kitchen.

Lard versus Vegetable Oil

The pre-Columbian people of Mexico did not cook food in fat or oil. Their clay cooking vessels could not have withstood temperatures necessary for frying, nor did they possess oil or fat in sufficient quantities to make the technique practical.

Spaniards introduced cooking fat (lard), along with pigs, cows, sheep, goats, and cheese, to Mexico after the Spanish Conquest in the early 16th century. It could be argued that the most revolutionary of these products was lard because it fundamentally changed the way the Mexican people prepared their food. By the end of the Colonial period (1650–1810), lard had become a staple in virtually every Mexican kitchen.

In recent decades however, the use of lard has fallen into disrepute in many world cuisines including that of Mexico. The word itself has become synonymous with being unhealthy and overweight. Many Mexican restaurants advertise that they don't use lard, though many substitutes, such as hydrogenated vegetable oils that contain transfats, can be less healthy than the natural animal fat they replace. This is because transfats not only raise "bad" cholesterol levels in the body, as do all saturated fats; they also lower "good" cholesterol levels.[1]

Admittedly, fat is a controversial topic. Saturated fats of any kind—including animal fats, hydrogenated fats, and even coconut and palm oil—are not as healthy as mono- and polyunsaturated fats such as olive oil and safflower oil. Lard contains 5 grams of saturated fat and 12 milligrams of cholesterol per tablespoon (15 grams), whereas most vegetable oils only contain 1 or 2 grams of saturated fat and no cholesterol.

But in its defense, pure rendered lard actually has less total fat per tablespoon (13 grams) than the average vegetable oil (15 grams), as well as lower overall calories (115 calories per tablespoon for lard compared to 119 for safflower oil).

So it probably comes down to how much lard is used and how often. Unless an individual is on a restricted diet because of health reasons, the occasional use of a small amount of lard in a recipe is probably not harmful. And for certain applications, no other fat has the authenticity, flavor, and mouth feel that lard provides. It should be noted, however, that there is a big difference between manufactured hydrogenated lard (those room temperature boxes sold at grocery stores) and lard that is pure and freshly rendered.

How to Render Lard

Yields 4 cups (1 liter)

Ingredients:

* 2 pounds (907 grams) pork fat, well chilled

Directions:

* Lard may be rendered on a stovetop or in the oven. If cooking in the oven, preheat to 325°F (163°C).

* Cut the fat into pieces and run it through a meat grinder; or cut into small dice, place in a food processor 1 cup at a time, and pulse until finely minced.

* If cooking on a stove, place the fat in a heavy pot or Dutch oven over medium heat and cook, stirring and scraping the bottom of the pan occasionally, until the clear fat is rendered, about a half hour.

* If cooking in an oven, place the Dutch oven on middle rack of a preheated oven until the fat has rendered.

* Strain, cover, and refrigerate until needed. (It will keep for several months under refrigeration.)

Notes: *Do not let the fat cook so long that it darkens in color.*

Once refrigerated and firm, the lard should be creamy white.

PART 2:
Fundamentals

Homemade Tortillas

White Wings Corn Tortilla mix (Harina para Preparada Tortillas de Maíz), which is manufactured by C.H. Guenther & Son, Inc. at Pioneer Mills in San Antonio, is our preferred brand of dried masa to use for making tortillas. Maseca Instant Corn Masa is also good and is widely available at many Mexican specialty stores and supermarkets nationwide. (If buying Maseca, be sure to buy the package that is labeled "Masa Instantánea de Maíz," which means "instant corn masa flour," not "para hacer tamales," which is intended for use in making tamales.) If buying another brand of dried masa, make sure the label reads "de maíz," which means corn.

Fresh masa is corn that has been nixtamalized and ground while still moist. It is packaged in plastic bags and sold by weight.

How to Make Tortillas Using Dried Masa

Yields 16 tortillas

Equipment:

* Tortilla press
* Comal or iron griddle

Ingredients:

* 2 cups (280 grams) Pioneer White Wings Corn Tortilla mix or Maseca Instant Corn Masa
* Kosher salt to taste (optional)

Directions:

* Cut rounds from plastic to fit the tortilla press. (This is a great way to reuse a plastic grocery bag.)

* Heat a well-seasoned comal or iron griddle over medium-high heat. If possible, set the comal at two temperatures: 325°F (163°C) and 375°F (191°C). The cooler side is for the first two turns of the tortilla. For the last turn of the tortilla, move it to the 375°F (191°C) side. This helps encourage puffing. Some chefs lay a tortilla directly on a burner flame for the last turn.

* Place the dried masa in a large bowl and slowly add 1⅓ cups (316 ml) warm water while stirring. Knead dough until it comes together. Add a little more water, 1 tablespoon (15 ml) at a time, or sprinkle on a little additional dried masa as needed to form a smooth, soft, moist dough (amount will vary depending on humidity and dryness of masa). Season with (optional) salt to taste. Let the dough rest for at least 30 minutes (to fully hydrate the dough), or refrigerate for several hours or overnight. If it has been refrigerated, allow the dough to sit at room temperature for about 1 hour before proceeding.

* Divide dough into 16 balls (see note) and cover with plastic wrap or a damp towel to prevent the dough from drying out (this is very important).

* Place a round of plastic on the tortilla press, and place a ball of masa on top of the plastic just slightly off center toward the hinge (this helps maintain an even thickness).

* Place a second piece of plastic over the ball of masa, flatten it slightly by hand, then close the lid and press.

* Some chefs like to turn the package 180 degrees and gently press again.

* With the tortilla still pressed between the plastic sheets, place in one hand and use other to peel off the top sheet of plastic. (Plastic sheets may be reused to make remaining tortillas.)

* Transfer the exposed side of tortilla to the opposite hand. Fingers should be close together and the tortilla should be placed on the fingertips, not the palm. Peel off the remaining sheet of plastic.

* Keeping palm up and nearly flat, gently lay the tortilla on the cooler side of the comal or iron griddle. Try to prevent the tortilla from folding over on itself when placing it on the comal. Cook for about 30 seconds, or until edges begin to firm.

* Using a thin spatula, turn tortilla. Cook for about 1 minute more; the underside should begin to develop little blisters and slight freckles of brown.

* Turn the tortilla over onto the hotter side of the comal, and after a few seconds, if the dough was the right consistency and the comal set to the right heat, the tortilla should puff up (if it doesn't, it is still perfectly usable). Continue cooking until the underside has some brown spots and the tortilla is cooked through.

* Place in a cloth-lined basket and keep covered while pressing and cooking the remaining tortillas.

Notes: *It is a good idea to do a test with the first tortilla before dividing dough into balls. The tortilla should be of even thickness—not so thin that it will tear apart when removed from the plastic, and not so thick that it will be difficult to fold or roll after it is cooked. The edge should be smooth, not crumbly. If it is crumbly, work a little more water into the dough.*

The dough should leave a little residue when pressed against the palm. Resist the temptation to wash off the thin film of dried masa that builds up on palms while transferring the tortillas to the comal. It actually helps keep the tortillas from sticking to hands.

How to Make Tortillas Using Fresh Masa

Yields 16 tortillas

Masa is a dough made from freshly ground nixtamalized corn (hominy).

Equipment:

* Tortilla press
* Comal or iron griddle

Ingredients:

* 1 ⅓ pounds (600 grams) fresh white corn masa
* Kosher salt to taste (optional)

Directions:

* Place the masa in a bowl and knead until it is smooth and soft; if it crumbles or breaks into pieces, add warm water, 1 tablespoon (15 ml) at a time, while kneading until the dough is the consistency of Play-Doh. It should be very soft and the edges of the dough should look smooth when pressed. Season with (optional) salt to taste.
* Form and cook the tortillas following the instructions for pressing tortillas using dried masa (see page 48).

Notes: Fresh masa turns sour after a day or two in the refrigerator. To extend the shelf life, masa can be divided into recipe-sized portions and frozen.

The dough should be as hydrated, soft, and pliable as possible without falling apart or sticking to hands. If it crumbles, it is too dry—add a little more water.

Opposite: dried corn kernels (center), nixtamalized corn (left), and fresh masa dough (lower right)

Colored Tortillas

Colored tortillas not only enhance the appearance of many enchilada recipes, but they also can heighten flavor, depending on the herb, chile, or vegetable used for the color. The tortillas are made with the same method used to make tortillas with dried masa. The ratio of liquid will be a little less than 1:1 ratio of volume measure to dried masa. For chile-infused tortillas, it's best not to dry roast the chiles. Fresh chiles will ensure the color remains as bright as possible.

How to Make Red Tortillas

Yields 12–15 tortillas

Ingredients:

* 2–4 ancho or guajillo chiles, cleaned, destemmed, deseeded
* Pinch of kosher salt
* 1 ½ cups (210 grams) dried masa

Directions:

* Place the chiles in a bowl and cover with hot water. Soak about 10 minutes, or until softened. Drain and discard the soaking liquid.
* Place softened chiles in a blender along with salt and 1 cup (237 ml) warm water. Process until smooth.
* Strain through a medium-mesh strainer into a large bowl.
* Add the dried masa and knead until the chile purée is evenly distributed through the dough. While kneading, add water as needed (approximately ¼ cup, 59 ml) to form a soft, workable dough.
* Let the dough rest a few minutes before dividing into balls and pressing. Follow the instructions for pressing tortillas using dried masa (see page 48).

Note: Red tortillas are used with Tex-Mex, Potosinas, Rioverdenses, and Tultecas Enchiladas.

How to Make Green Tortillas

Yields 12–15 tortillas

Ingredients:

* 1 bunch cilantro, washed, patted dry

* Pinch of kosher salt

* 1 ½ cups (210 grams) dried masa

Directions:

* Trim and discard 1–2 inches (2.5–5 cm) from the root end of the cilantro stems.

* Place the cilantro in a blender along with salt and 1 cup (237 ml) warm water. Process until smooth.

* Strain through a medium-mesh strainer into a large bowl.

* Add dried masa and knead until the cilantro purée is evenly distributed throughout the dough. While kneading, add water as needed (approximately ¼ cup, 59 ml) to make a soft, workable dough.

* Let the dough rest a few minutes before dividing into balls and pressing. Follow the instructions for pressing tortillas using dried masa (see page 48).

Note: Green tortillas work especially well with chicken, vegetable, and cheese fillings.

How to Make Black Bean Tortillas

Yields approximately 12–15 tortillas

Ingredients:

* Approximately 1 cup (240 grams) cooked black beans (see page 60)

* Pinch of kosher salt

* 1 tablespoon (15 ml) vegetable oil (see note)

* 1 ½ cups (210 grams) dried masa

Directions:

* Place cooked black beans in a blender along with salt, oil, and 1 cup (237 ml) warm water. Pulse until the beans are broken up and mostly puréed (a little texture is desirable).

* Place in a large bowl, add the dried masa, and knead until the beans are evenly distributed throughout dough. While kneading, add water as needed (approximately ¼ cup, 59 ml, see note) to make a soft, workable dough.

* Let the dough rest a few minutes before dividing into balls and pressing. Follow the instructions for pressing tortillas using dried masa (see page 48).

Notes: *The oil is added to help keep the edges of bean tortillas from cracking.*

Since the moisture content of cooked beans is difficult to predict, the amount of water needed for the recipe will vary. Try to attain a very soft but workable dough. If the edges of a pressed tortilla crack or appear serrated, add a little more water, a few drops at a time, to achieve the right consistency.

For a more rustic appearance, simply mash the beans by hand before adding water and dried masa. Black bean tortillas work well with almost any meat, cheese, or vegetable filling.

Other Colored Tortillas

Red beets, spinach, tomato paste, huitlacoche, and herbs are just a few examples of other ingredients that can be incorporated into masa dough to add color and flavor to tortillas. Experiment using the approximate ratio of 1 $\frac{1}{2}$ parts dried masa to 1–1 $\frac{1}{4}$ parts puréed coloring ingredient. Pair the flavor profile of the tortilla with the flavor of the dominant ingredient in the filling.

Store-Bought Tortillas

There is nothing better than a fresh, handmade tortilla. It has a tender, melt-in-the-mouth quality and a delicious hominy corn flavor that doesn't call for any embellishment besides a swipe of butter or a dip of salsa.

Tortillas of this quality take great skill to make and are difficult to find, which may explain why flour tortillas have gained so much popularity in Mexican recipes. But flour tortillas are not appropriate for enchiladas.

Fortunately, it is possible to make good enchiladas with store-bought corn tortillas. If the tortillas are a day old, they are still perfectly useable and can even make the job of preparing enchiladas easier, because an extremely fresh tortilla will quickly fall apart when softened in hot oil or a sauce.

In many cities, tortillas made from white or yellow corn are available, and both make excellent enchiladas. Red tortillas are the traditional choice for recipes such as Tex-Mex enchiladas served with chile gravy. Unfortunately, commercially made red tortillas add color and nothing more to the dish—originally, their rosy hue came from chile paste mixed into the masa, but today it comes from food coloring.

When shopping for commercially made tortillas, avoid the frozen kind, which tend to be leathery. A local Mexican grocery store usually offers reliable brands and has a quick turnover that improves the odds of the tortillas being fresh. Avoid more expensive "artisan" tortillas as they are often too thick to make a tender enchilada.

Fire Roasting Fresh Chiles

The purpose of fire roasting fresh chiles, such as poblanos, is to facilitate removal of the skin and to enhance the chile's flavor. Do not cook the chile; only blacken the skin. There are several methods used to accomplish this.

Method 1:

Place whole chiles directly on a barbeque grill over hot coals or a gas flame. Turn the chiles to blacken them evenly. This is a particularly effective method for quickly blackening without overcooking. When chiles are evenly blistered and blackened, remove and place them in a paper bag. Place the paper bag inside a plastic bag, close, and allow the chiles to steam for several minutes or until they are cool enough to handle. (An alternate method of steaming chiles is to place them on a plate and cover with a large bowl.) When cool, the skins should easily slip off the chiles. Remove the stems, veins, and seeds. To maintain maximum flavor, chiles should not be rinsed with water.

Method 2:

Line a cookie sheet with aluminum foil to facilitate cleanup. Rub the whole chiles with a little oil and spread them out in a single layer on the cookie sheet. Place under a broiler a few inches away from the heat source.

Turn the chiles every few minutes to evenly blacken and blister the skins. Proceed with steaming and cleaning chiles as described in Method 1. This is an easy way to process a large number of chiles that will be used in a sauce. It is not the best way to fire roast chiles to use as strips (rajas) or to stuff (rellenos), because the heat of an oven tends to cook chiles and make them soft.

Method 3:

Place a chile directly over a high flame on a gas stove, turning with tongs until it is blackened (a barbeque grate placed over the burner is a big help). The chile can also be held over a flame using tongs or by piercing the stem end with a meat fork. Proceed with steaming and cleaning the chiles as described in Method 1.

Method 4:

Chef Iliana de la Vega says deep frying or pan frying chiles in oil just long enough to blister their skins is another option, but the oil will turn dark and cannot be used to cook anything else.

Note: *Remember, it is important to avoid cooking the chile—only blacken the skin.*

Dried Chiles

Dried chiles must be cleaned, dry roasted on a comal or iron griddle, rehydrated, and puréed before use in enchilada recipes. The purpose of dry roasting chiles is to caramelize the sugars and release the aromatic oils—not to fully cook them.

How to Prepare Dried Chiles

Directions:

* Wipe each chile with a damp cloth to remove any dust.

* Using a knife or scissors, cut a slit down the side and remove the seeds, veins, and stem. (It saves cleanup to do this over a sink or bowl to catch the seeds.) Tear the chile into manageable pieces. Repeat with remaining chiles.

* With tongs in one hand and a spatula in the other, place a piece of prepared chile on a well-seasoned, unoiled comal or iron griddle over medium heat (comal should not be extremely hot, which would burn the chile and make the sauce bitter). Press on the chile with spatula for a few seconds while holding it in place with tongs. The inside flesh should turn a medium brown color. The skin may or may not blister, depending on amount of moisture in the chile. Turn the chile over and repeat the process on the other side, being careful not to scorch it. Transfer to a bowl, and roast the remaining chile pieces.

* When all chile pieces have been roasted, add enough hot water to cover and soak for a few minutes until soft (approximately 15 minutes, depending on how dry the chiles are).

* Unless instructed otherwise in a specific recipe, discard the soaking liquid. Place reconstituted chiles in a blender along with a small amount of fresh water (or broth, if called for), and purée to a smooth consistency. Strain the chile purée through a medium-mesh strainer before proceeding with a recipe.

Notes: *Do not soak the chiles too long or they will lose flavor.*

The soaking liquid is usually discarded—it can be bitter and may contain impurities such as residual pesticides.

Chef Victor Maldonado says when processing dry roasted chiles with other ingredients in a blender, always put the chiles in the blender first. This helps them more fully incorporate into the sauce.

Dry Roasting Tomatoes, Onions, Garlic, and Fresh Chiles

Dry roasting tomatoes, onions, garlic, and small fresh chiles, such as jalapeños and serranos, brings out their sweetness, softens harsh raw flavors, and adds depth to enchilada sauces.

Directions:

* It is not necessary to peel fruits and vegetables before roasting. Roma tomatoes, cloves garlic, and chiles are left whole. Onions are simply cut in half or quartered.

* Place an unoiled comal, iron griddle, or heavy skillet over medium-high heat.

* When hot, place the fruits and vegetables to be roasted on the comal.

* As they begin to brown and blacken in spots, turn and continue cooking until they are slightly softened and evenly colored.

* The garlic will be ready first—when it has a few brown spots and has begun to soften, remove and set aside. Serranos, tomatoes, and onions are ready when they blister and blacken in spots and become slightly soft.

* When cool, garlic should be peeled. Remove the root and stem end of the onion and any papery outer layers of skin. Tomatoes are sometimes peeled, sometimes not, depending on whether the smoky flavor of the skins is desired in the sauce. It is not necessary to peel or deseed small chiles after roasting. Simply remove the stem.

Dried Beans

Many varieties of dried beans are used in Mexican cuisine, but two of the most popular are pinto and black turtle beans. Both are prepared similarly and can often be substituted for each other.

How to Prepare Dried Beans

Yields 6 cups (1.36 kilos) cooked beans

Ingredients:

* 1 pound (454 grams) dried beans, 2–2 ½ cups
* Kosher salt as needed
* 1 medium white onion, peeled and chopped
* 1 large clove garlic, peeled and minced
* 1 tablespoon (15 grams) lard or vegetable oil

Optional ingredients:

* 1 dried avocado leaf (see page 17) or
* 1 sprig epazote (see page 39) or
* 1 teaspoon (1 gram) dried Mexican oregano (see page 39)
* 1 teaspoon fresh or dried chile pequín (1 gram), finely minced (or substitute other chiles such as serrano or jalapeño)

Directions:

* Spread the beans out on a cookie sheet. Sort and discard any broken or discolored beans as well as any pebbles or little clumps of dirt. Rinse thoroughly.
* Place the beans in a deep pot (an earthenware bean pot is optimal, but a stainless steel stockpot works fine) and cover with plenty of water.
* Add about 3 tablespoons (27 grams) kosher salt. (It is true that beans cooked in salted water never get tender. But soaking beans in cold salted water, then draining and rinsing before cooking, will result in a better overall texture and softened skins when the beans are fully cooked.)
* Soak the beans in the refrigerator for several hours or overnight.
* Drain and rinse the soaked beans at least twice, then cover with fresh water by about 2 inches (5 cm). Do not add any salt at this time.
* Bring the beans to a boil, then reduce heat to a simmer. Skim off the foam that rises to the surface.
* When all foam has been removed, add the chopped onion and garlic.
* Simmer uncovered about 2 hours, or until tender, adding water as necessary to keep the beans barely covered with liquid.
* When the beans are tender, salt to taste and stir in the lard or vegetable oil.

* Continue cooking until the beans are very tender and broth slightly thickened.
* An avocado leaf, epazote sprig, Mexican oregano, or chile may be added during the last half hour of cooking.

Alternate Methods

* To save time, skip the long soak in salt water. Instead, place rinsed and sorted beans in a pot, cover with water, and bring to a rapid boil. Remove from heat, cover, and soak for 1 hour.
* Rinse, cover with fresh water by about 2 inches (5 cm), and proceed with the directions for cooking beans.
* Some cooks recommend that beans should not be soaked at all, but cooked immediately after sorting and rinsing. Beans can be prepared this way, but soaking and rinsing removes some of the indigestible starches, making the beans more palatable.
* A pressure cooker will cook beans in a matter of minutes, but care must be taken to cover the beans with plenty of water and to allow the cooker to naturally depressurize before opening or the beans will tend to burst. Some depth of flavor is lost with this method.
* Beans can also be soaked and then cooked in a ceramic-lined slow cooker.

Refried Beans

Refried beans are a mainstay of the Mexican kitchen and may be served at any or every meal of the day. Lard is essential for authentic flavor, but vegetable oils may be substituted (see page 44).

How to Make Refried Beans

Yields about 3 cups (780 grams)

Ingredients:

* 4 cups (1 liter) cooked pinto or black beans, with broth (see page 60)
* ¼–⅓ cup (56–70 grams) lard or ¼ cup (59 ml) vegetable oil
* 1–2 tablespoons (10–20 grams) white onion, finely minced
* Kosher salt to taste

Directions:

* Place the lard or oil in a large, heavy frying pan over medium heat.
* Add the onion and sauté 3–5 minutes, until translucent, 3–5 minutes.
* Increase heat to medium-high and add the beans. Then add the broth, 1 cup (237 ml) at a time, mashing, stirring, and reducing until the beans have been incorporated.
* Lower heat to medium and continue cooking, constantly scraping the bottom and sides of the pan to prevent scorching, until the beans are reduced to a thick paste. Season with salt to taste.

Notes: For use as a sauce in the Enfrijolada recipe, the refried beans are thinned with additional bean broth or water to a sauce consistency.

If preparing beans ahead of time, transfer to a microwavable container, cool for a few minutes, place plastic wrap in contact with surface of beans to prevent formation of a crust, cover, and refrigerate.

To reheat, remove the plastic wrap from the surface of the beans, cover the bowl with fresh plastic wrap, and microwave at medium power, stirring occasionally, until thoroughly reheated.

Refried beans can also be reheated on a stovetop over medium-low heat. Add a small amount of water (depending on thickness of the paste) and stir continuously until heated through.

Refried beans also freeze well.

Mexican Rice

Rice was brought to Mexico in the early 16th century by the Spanish, who had been introduced to it by Moorish invaders eight centuries before (the Spanish word for rice, *arroz*, was derived from the Arabic word *al rruz*).

Because of that history, it should not be surprising that the names "Mexican Rice" and "Spanish Rice" often conjure up a picture of a dish somewhat like paella or Middle Eastern pilaf—reddish orange or yellow grains richly flavored with onions, tomatoes, spices, mild chiles, vegetables, and stock. This is the common way rice is served in Mexican restaurants in the United States, but it is not the only way Mexicans prepare it.

In Mexico, rice is served many ways, from a cinnamon- and almond-flavored drink called horchata, to desserts, like arroz con leche. Rice is often an ingredient in sopas secas ("dry soups," where the liquid is absorbed by the rice) and sopas aguadas (literally, "wet soups").

When served as a side dish, flavor components added to the rice are usually dictated by the main course. The rice may be colored red from the addition of achiote (annatto seed), dried red chiles, or tomato purée, green from poblano chiles and cilantro, brown from bean purée, or plain white. The rice can be flecked with herbs, whole beans, and corn or other vegetables, and it can be simmered in meat stock, a flavorful liquid, or plain water.

Mexicans use both short grain (Morelos) and long grain (Sinaloa) rice. The following recipes call for long grain rice. A heavy saucepan with a well-fitting lid is essential for the rice to turn out well. Once the lid is in place, it should not be removed until the cooking time has elapsed. The rice should also rest before serving for half the time it was cooked (for example, rice cooked 20 minutes should rest 10). And though rice will cook well on a stovetop, many professional chefs suggest that it is even easier to bake rice in a 375°F (191°C) oven.

How to Make Mexican White Rice

Yields 8–10 cups (2–2.5 liters)

This recipe produces tender, creamy rice that is the perfect accompaniment for highly seasoned or complex dishes. It is also a good foundation for adding other ingredients. (See Primavera Rice recipe, next page.)

Ingredients:

* ½ cup (118 ml) vegetable oil
* 2 cups (360 grams) long grain white rice
* ⅓ cup (47 grams) onion, small dice
* 1 tablespoon (7 grams) garlic, minced
* 1 tablespoon (9 grams) kosher salt
* 2 tablespoons (56 grams) unsalted butter, cut into ½-inch (12 mm) pieces

Directions (oven method):

* Preheat the oven to 375°F (191°C).
* Place oil in a 4 quart (4 liter) saucepan over medium-high heat.
* Add the rice and onion and sauté, stirring frequently, until the onion is translucent, 3–5 minutes.
* Add garlic and sauté for 1 additional minute.
* Add 4 cups (1 liter) water and salt.
* Bring to a boil, reduce heat to a low simmer, cover, and place in a preheated 375°F (191°C) oven for approximately 20 minutes, or until the liquid is absorbed.
* Add butter, fluff the rice with a fork, cover, and let rest 10 minutes before serving.

Note: The rice can also be cooked for the same length of time on a stovetop, but pay close attention to the heat level to avoid boiling over or scorching.

How to Make Cilantro Rice

Yields 8–10 cups (2–2.5 liters)

This rice is the perfect accompaniment for Enchiladas de Barbacoa (see page 124).

Directions:

* Follow the steps above for Mexican White Rice, but instead of adding 4 cups (1 liter) water to the saucepan, purée 1 small bunch cilantro in a blender with 3 cups (710 ml) water. Add additional water as needed to equal 4 cups (1 liter) total and use this as the cooking liquid for the rice.
* If desired, add 1 cup (135 grams) fresh or frozen corn kernels right after the rice finishes cooking. Residual heat from the rice as it rests will cook the corn.

How to Make Primavera Rice

Yields about 10–12 cups (2.5 –3 liters)

Ingredients:

* 1 recipe Mexican White Rice (see previous page)
* 1 cup (140 grams) nopalitos (cactus paddles), small dice
* ½ cup (68 grams) frozen corn kernels
* ½ cup frozen peas (65 grams)
* 1 cup (140 grams) carrots, peeled, small dice
* 1 cup (140 grams) zucchini, small dice
* 1 cup (200 grams) Roma tomatoes, cored, deseeded, and finely chopped
* Kosher salt and black pepper to taste

Directions:

* Massage the diced nopalitos with kosher salt, place in a colander, and let rest for a half hour. Rinse thoroughly and pat dry before using.
* Measure the corn and peas and set out at room temperature.
* Place the carrots in a saucepan, cover with water, and bring to a boil.
* Add the zucchini, turn off heat, cover, and let sit for about 10 minutes, or until tender. Drain and pat the vegetables dry.
* Immediately after the rice is cooked, gently fold in the prepared vegetables and tomatoes.
* Taste and adjust the seasoning. Cover and let rest 10 minutes before serving.

How to Make Moros y Cristianos (Whole Black Beans and Rice)

Yields about 10 cups (2.5 liters)

The name for this rice has its roots in Spanish history, when the Moors conquered and occupied Spain—it means "Moors and Christians."

Ingredients:

* 1 recipe Mexican White Rice (see previous page)
* 2 cups (480 grams) cooked black beans (see page 60)

Directions:

* Place the black beans in a sieve, rinse with warm water, and gently blot dry with paper towels (this helps preserve the white color of the rice).
* Immediately after the rice is cooked, gently fold in the beans.
* Cover and let rest for 10 minutes before serving.

How to Make Black Bean Rice

Yields 10 cups (2.5 liters)

Ingredients:

* 2 cups (480 grams) cooked black beans, drained (see page 60)
* 5 cups (1.185 liters) water or vegetable stock
* 1 tablespoon (9 grams) kosher salt
* ½ cup (118 ml) vegetable oil
* 2 cups (360 grams) long grain white rice
* ⅓ cup (47 grams) onion, small dice
* 1 serrano chile, destemmed and minced (optional)
* 1 tablespoon (7 grams) garlic, minced
* 1 sprig epazote or 1 avocado leaf (optional)

Directions:

* Preheat the oven to 375°F (191°C).
* Place the beans, water or stock, and salt in a blender and purée until smooth.
* Place the oil in a 4 quart (4 liter) saucepan over medium-high heat.
* Add the rice, onion, and serrano chile (if using) and sauté, stirring frequently, until the onion is translucent, 3–5 minutes.
* Add the garlic and sauté for an additional minute.
* Stir in the bean purée.
* Add a sprig of epazote or an avocado leaf (if using).
* Bring to a simmer, cover, and bake in the oven for approximately 20 minutes, or until the liquid is absorbed.
* Remove from heat, discard the epazote sprig or avocado leaf, fluff with a fork, cover, and let rest 10 minutes before serving.

Note: The rice may also be cooked for the same amount of time on a stovetop, but pay close attention to the heat level to avoid boiling over or scorching.

How to Make Mexican Red Rice

Yields about 10 cups (2.5 liters)

This is the style of rice typically associated with Mexican food restaurants in the United States.

Ingredients:

* ¹⁄₂ cup (118 ml) vegetable oil
* 2 cups (360 grams) long grain white rice
* ¹⁄₃ cup (47 grams) onion, small dice
* ¹⁄₃ cup (47 grams) poblano chile, destemmed, deseeded, small dice (see note)
* 3 dried guajillo chiles, destemmed, deveined, and deseeded (see note)
* 1 tablespoon (7 grams) minced garlic
* 4 cups (1 liter) chicken stock
* Dehydrated chicken or vegetable bouillon to taste

Directions:

* Preheat the oven to 375°F (191°C).
* Place the oil in a 4 quart (4 liter) saucepan over medium-high heat.
* Add the rice, onion, and poblano chile. Sauté, stirring frequently, until the onion is translucent, 3–5 minutes.
* Place the guajillo chiles, garlic, and stock in a blender and process until the chiles are liquefied.
* Stir the blended ingredients into the rice mixture. Add bouillon to taste (the liquid should be somewhat salty).
* Bring to a simmer, cover, and bake in the oven for approximately 20 minutes, or until the liquid is absorbed.
* Remove from heat, fluff with a fork, cover, and let rest 10 minutes before serving.

Note: Chiles do not need to be dry roasted or fire roasted for this recipe.

The rice may also be cooked for the same amount of time on a stovetop, but pay close attention to the heat level to avoid boiling over or scorching.

Tips on Making Mexican Rice

When adding canned tomatoes to a rice recipe, be sure to drain off the watery liquid. (The liquid may be used as part of the cooking liquid if desired, but for best results, be sure to include it as part of the total measurement of liquid required.)

A meat fork is the perfect tool for fluffing rice without damaging the grains.

Poached Chicken for Enchiladas

French author, chef, and restaurateur Auguste Escoffier described poaching as a "boiling that does not boil." This is a good description of the optimum way to cook chicken for use in enchilada recipes because it guarantees that the meat remains tender, flavorful, and moist.

How to Poach Chicken for Use in Enchiladas

Yields approximately 5 cups (650 grams) shredded chicken

Equipment:

* Deep soup pot with lid
* Calibrated instant-read thermometer

Ingredients:

* 3 pounds (1.36 kilos) chicken pieces, bone in, skin on, white or dark meat, or a mixture of both (depending on what the recipe calls for)
* 4 teaspoons (12 grams) kosher salt
* 1 medium white onion, peeled and quartered
* 2 cloves garlic, peeled and slightly crushed
* 8 whole peppercorns

Directions:

* Remove the chicken pieces from the refrigerator approximately 1 hour before poaching. Separate thighs and legs; if breasts are very thick or large, cut in half.
* Place 3 quarts (3 liters) water in a deep soup pot over high heat. Add salt, onion, garlic, and peppercorns and bring to a boil. Lower heat slightly, cover, and let boil for about 15 minutes to infuse water with the seasonings.
* Add the chicken (legs and thighs first, followed by the breasts) and allow the liquid to return almost to a boil.
* Immediately adjust heat to the barest simmer (just an occasional bubble) 195–205°F (91–96°C) and allow chicken to poach until the meat reaches an internal temperature of 165°F (74°C). Begin checking internal temperature of smaller pieces at 25 minutes—cooking times for individual pieces will vary. Large or thick breast pieces may take up to 1 hour, but be careful not to overcook or boil.
* As the chicken pieces are done, remove them from the pot, moisten with broth, and allow to cool.
* When cool enough to handle, shred the chicken into bite-size pieces (*deshebrada*), discarding skin and bones.
* Sprinkle with a little more broth, cover, and refrigerate until needed.

Note: *The remaining broth can be reduced, strained, degreased, and frozen for other uses, such as in soups or rice, or for poaching.*

Simmered Pork or Beef for Enchiladas

Beef and pork are popular as fillings for enchiladas and are usually prepared the same way, by gently braising in a flavorful liquid. The secret is to simmer, not boil, the meat just until it is fork-tender. (In other words, when a meat fork is inserted into a piece of meat, it slips easily off the fork.) Be careful not to cook beef or pork so long that it becomes mushy. It is also helpful to cut meat into 2–4 inch (5–10 cm) pieces with, not against, the grain. This shortens cooking time and makes shredding easier.

How to Prepare Pork or Beef for Use in Enchiladas

Yields approximately 2 cups (260 grams) shredded pork or beef

Equipment:

* Deep saucepan or soup pot

Ingredients:

* 1 pound (454 grams) pork shoulder or beef chuck
* 1 small white onion, peeled and cut in half
* 2 cloves garlic, peeled and slightly crushed
* Kosher or sea salt as needed

Directions:

* Cut the meat into smaller chunks or pieces with, not against, grain.
* Place meat, onion, and garlic in a soup pot. It is not necessary to brown meat.
* Add enough cold water to cover and salt—approximately 1 teaspoon (5 ml) per quart of liquid.
* Bring just to a boil over high heat and immediately reduce heat to a simmer.
* Skim any foam that rises to the surface. (Move the saucepan partially off the burner to create a convection boil; this pushes impurities to one side of the pan, making removal of foam easier.)
* Cook until the meat is fork-tender, 1–1 $^1/_2$ hours.
* If time permits, allow the meat to cool in cooking liquid.
* When cool enough to handle, shred the chicken into bite-size pieces (*deshebrada*) using two forks or hands.
* Moisten with a little cooking liquid, cover, and refrigerate until needed.

Note: *The broth can be defatted, strained, and used to enrich enchilada sauce, or refrigerated or frozen for other uses, such as in rice dishes or soups.*

The Enchilada Assembly

Anyone who has ever breaded a pork chop or fish fillet to prepare it for pan frying knows how much it helps to have the dishes of flour, egg, and breadcrumbs lined up side by side so the food can be prepared in an assembly-line fashion.

The same assembly-line method is used when making enchiladas, but with the additional challenge of working at a stove. And because enchiladas are assembled just before serving, the task has to be accomplished quickly and efficiently to keep everything warm.

There are two basic methods for preparing a tortilla for use in an enchilada recipe—by frying the tortilla in oil and then dipping it in a sauce, or by dipping the tortilla in a sauce and then frying it in oil. Whichever method the recipe calls for, have the sauce, filling, garnishes, and serving platter, casserole, or individual plates ready before proceeding.

The sauce should be kept warm in a skillet over low heat. A bowl or saucepan holding the warmed filling ingredients should be nearby. A warm plate is needed for filling and rolling (or folding) the tortillas. Serving dishes should be warmed and ready for plating the completed enchiladas. All garnishes should be prepped and at hand to complete the dish. Unless instructed otherwise, enchiladas are always served immediately after they are assembled.

Method 1: Fry the tortillas in oil and then dip in sauce

Place $1/2$ inch (12 mm) oil or lard in a small saucepan over medium heat. Have a sheet tray ready and lined with paper towels.

One at a time, gently fry each tortilla for a few seconds per side until it begins to soften. Some Mexican chefs say to "pass the tortilla through the oil," which is a good description of the timing of the procedure. Be careful not to fry the tortilla so long that the edges begin to brown or it begins to crisp. Place the softened tortilla on the paper towels to drain for a few moments. Repeat with the other tortillas. Do not leave the softened tortillas for too long or they will begin to harden.

Working quickly, dip a softened tortilla in the warm sauce. (Some chefs do not completely immerse the tortilla in the sauce, but simply spoon a little sauce on the inside of the tortilla before adding the filling. This is quicker and neater, especially when working in a busy restaurant.)

Place a couple of tablespoons of filling on the lower third of the sauced tortilla, roll or fold as instructed in the recipe, and place on a warmed platter, casserole, or an individual serving plate. Repeat with the remaining tortillas.

When the enchiladas have been plated, garnish and serve immediately. (The only exception to this is when a recipe calls for placing the completed platter or casserole of enchiladas under a broiler for a few minutes to melt cheese or to lightly brown a topping, such as for Enchiladas Suizas.)

Lower calorie options:

If the tortillas are fresh enough, they can simply be dipped in the sauce. They can also be softened on a comal that has been lightly sprayed with cooking spray or by wiping the comal's surface with a paper towel dipped in a little oil.

Method 2: Dip the tortillas in sauce and then fry

As in the previous method, have the sauce, filling, serving pieces, and garnishes ready before proceeding.

The sauce should be in a skillet or sauté pan over low heat. In a sauté pan on an adjoining burner, place ¼ inch (6 mm) of oil or lard over medium (not high) heat.

To facilitate cleanup, place aluminum foil on the stovetop surrounding the skillets or sauté pans and on the backsplash. A plate for filling and rolling (or folding) the enchiladas should be nearby, as well as the warm serving platter, casserole, or individual plates.

Test the temperature of the oil by taking an extra tortilla, dipping it in the sauce, and frying it. The oil should gently bubble and sizzle around the edges of the tortilla. Working one at a time, dip each tortilla in the sauce, let the excess drip back into the pan, and carefully place the sauced tortilla in the oil. Fry for a few seconds per side, and move to a warm plate. (A large slotted spatula is the perfect tool for handling tortillas prepared using this method.)

Place a couple of tablespoons of filling on the lower third of the sauced and fried tortilla, roll or fold as instructed in the recipe, and place on a warm serving platter or individual plate. Repeat with the other tortillas.

Notes: This method produces a caramelization of the sugars in the chiles, but it can also produce some pretty large splatters and pops as the sauced tortilla hits the hot oil, so be careful to keep the oil at a medium—not high—temperature.

With either method, when using individual serving plates, plan on 2–3 enchiladas per serving.

Tips on Garnishing

Celebratory colors abound in Mexico and permeate almost every aspect of life from gardens and architecture to paintings, potteries, and textiles, and of course the cuisine. From the contrasting salsas on top of Enchiladas Divorciadas to the vivid colors of the Mexican flag represented in Enchiladas Banderas, the appearance of Mexican food is every bit as vibrant as its flavor.

There's some truth to the old saying "We eat with our eyes first," and to please the eye as well as the palate takes an equal amount of thoughtful attentiveness and creativity. Nonfunctional garnishes, which are garnishes that may look pretty but add no flavor or benefit to a dish, should be avoided—especially when they conflict with the flavor of a dish, such as sprinkling cilantro haphazardly on top of a mole negro or using inedible garnishes such as dried bay leaves.

To avoid this problem, garnishes traditionally associated with a particular recipe are always a good place to start, such as the crumbled cheese, olives, capers, and sliced onion rings that are associated with Enchiladas Regias, or the cabbage slaw that goes so well with Enchiladas de Camarón.

Also, the way a garnish is handled can enhance or detract from a dish. Here are some examples:

* Cilantro is a very delicate herb, and rough treatment easily bruises and discolors the leaves—it should be lightly chopped with a sharp knife or whole individual leaves plucked from the stems right before being scattered over a dish.

* Capers are striking in appearance but also in flavor, and like all salty or strongly flavored garnishes, should be used sparingly.

* Jalapeños en escabeche (pickled) and fresh (raw) jalapeños have distinctly different flavors and are not interchangeable.

* Green olives are usualy called for in Mexican cuisine, so black olives are generally not a good substitute.

* Sliced onion rings are more visual than plain diced onions and give the guests the option of how little or how much onion they want to have with their serving. (And remember, white onions are preferred to yellow onions in Mexican cuisine because of their milder flavor.)

* Cheeses are a very popular topping, but try to pair the saltiness, texture, and melting quality of a cheese with the dish, especially when substituting one cheese for another.

* Dried herbs are usually not ideal for garnishing as they are too strong and dry.

* Napa cabbage is often a good garnish substitute for iceberg lettuce, because it is more durable.

* Finally, the saying "Less is more" is a good motto to adopt when it comes to the art of garnishing.

PART 3:
Recipes

Enchiladas Espinacas * PAGE 194

Accompaniments
Guarniciones

Roasted Tomato Salsa

Yields 4 cups (1 liter)

INGREDIENTS

* 1 ½ pounds (680 grams) ripe Roma tomatoes, cored but unpeeled
* ¼ medium yellow or white onion, unpeeled
* 3 serrano chiles, or to taste
* 2 cloves garlic, unpeeled
* Kosher salt to taste

DIRECTIONS

* Place the tomatoes, onion, chiles, and cloves garlic on an ungreased comal or iron griddle over medium-high heat.
* Remove the garlic when it just begins to have a few brown spots.
* Continue to cook the chiles, tomatoes, and onion until they begin to have numerous brown patches and are blackened in places.
* When the ingredients are cooked, remove the stems from the serrano chiles and the root end of onion, and peel the cloves of garlic.
* Place the ingredients in a blender and pulse to a rough salsa consistency. Do not overprocess. Season with salt to taste.

Note: Cover and refrigerate until needed. (Will keep, refrigerated, for five days.) Bring to room temperature before using.

Pico de Gallo

Yields about 2 cups (473 ml)

A generic term for various fresh salsas, pico de gallo *literally translates as "rooster's beak." This version pairs well with Enchiladas de Nopales (see page 208).*

INGREDIENTS

* 1 ½ cups (300 grams) Roma tomatoes, chopped
* 3 tablespoons (27 grams) white onion, small dice
* 2 tablespoons (1.5 grams) cilantro, minced
* 1–2 serrano chiles, or to taste
* 3 tablespoons (45 ml) lime juice
* Kosher salt to taste

DIRECTIONS

* Mix all ingredients together.
* Add salt to taste.

Black Bean Relish

Yields about 1 cup (237 ml)

This is used as a garnish for Enchiladas de Nopales.

INGREDIENTS

* ¼ cup (60 grams) cooked black beans, rinsed and chilled (see page 60)
* ¼ cup (40 grams) frozen corn kernels, defrosted
* ¼ cup (40 grams) red bell pepper, small dice
* ¼ cup (40 grams) red onion, small dice
* Handful cilantro, chopped
* Lime juice to taste
* Kosher salt to taste

DIRECTIONS

* Mix first five ingredients together.
* Add lime juice and salt to taste.

Cebolla Encurtida (Pickled Onion)

Yields about 1 cup (237 ml)

INGREDIENTS

* 1 medium red onion, peeled and thinly sliced
* Kosher salt to taste
* Juice of 6–7 limes

DIRECTIONS

* Place the onion in a nonreactive bowl.
* Season with salt and lime juice to taste.
* Mix well. Let sit for 15 minutes.
* Toss and allow to rest an additional 15 minutes before serving.

Romaine Lettuce Salad

Yields 4 cups (1 liter)

This is used as a garnish for La Fonda Enchiladas Suizas.

INGREDIENTS

* 6 large leaves romaine lettuce, ribs removed and shredded
* 2 medium tomatoes, cored, deseeded, and chopped
* 1 small serrano chile, destemmed, deseeded, and minced
* 4 green onions, chopped
* Cilantro sprigs to taste
* 1 teaspoon (5 ml) lime juice
* 2 teaspoons (10 ml) vegetable oil
* Kosher salt and ground black pepper to taste

DIRECTIONS

* Toss lettuce, tomatoes, serrano chile, green onions, and cilantro sprigs together. Cover and refrigerate until needed.
* Whisk the lime juice and oil together until emulsified. Add salt and pepper to taste. Cover and refrigerate until needed.
* Just before serving the enchiladas, pour the lime juice and oil dressing over salad and toss to mix. Taste and adjust the seasoning.

Nopalito Salad

Yields about 3 cups (710 ml)

INGREDIENTS

* 2 cups sliced nopalitos, rubbed well with kosher salt, rinsed, and patted dry (see page 20)
* 1 cup (237 ml) Pico de Gallo (see page 81)
* Kosher salt to taste

DIRECTIONS

* Combine the nopalitos and pico de gallo. Add salt to taste.

Napa Slaw

Yields about 3 cups (710 ml)

This is used as a garnish for Enchiladas de Playa and Enchiladas de Camarón.

INGREDIENTS

For the slaw:

* 2 cups (65 grams) napa cabbage, julienned
* ½ cup (15 grams) cilantro, minced
* ½ cup (30 grams) red radish, julienned

For the vinaigrette:

* 2 tablespoons (30 ml) red wine vinegar
* ¼ cup (59 ml) extra virgin olive oil
* Kosher salt and freshly ground black pepper to taste

DIRECTIONS

* Toss the cabbage, cilantro, and radish together. Cover and refrigerate.
* Whisk the olive oil into the vinegar and add salt and black pepper to taste. Cover and refrigerate.
* Just before serving, pour the dressing over the salad and toss to mix.
* Taste and adjust the seasoning.

Salsa Cruda (Tomatillo and Avocado Salsa)

Yields 1.5 cups (355 ml)

Any uncooked salsa may be called "salsa cruda," which indicates the sauce is not cooked. In San Antonio, salsa cruda is often made featuring tomatillos, avocado, serranos, and cilantro. The tomatillos are quite tart, so add the lime juice a little at a time until the flavors are balanced. The same is true regarding the spiciness of the serrano chile. It's best to add a little at a time until the desired level of heat is achieved.

INGREDIENTS

* 8 ounces (227 grams) tomatillos, husks removed, cored, and quartered
* 1–2 medium serrano chiles, destemmed and chopped, divided
* 2 medium cloves garlic, peeled and chopped
* ½ cup (14 grams) packed cilantro leaves
* 1 large avocado, peeled and deseeded
* Juice of ½ lime (2 teaspoons, 10 ml), or to taste
* Kosher salt to taste

DIRECTIONS

* Place the tomatillos, serrano chile (reserving some to add later as needed), garlic, cilantro, and avocado in a blender and process until smooth. Add salt and lime juice to taste and more serrano if desired.

* If a chunkier salsa is preferred, reserve a quarter of the avocado and 1 tomatillo. After the rest of the ingredients are processed, dice the reserved avocado and tomatillo and fold into the salsa. Taste and adjust the seasonings.

Note: *Salsa is best served the day it is made. It can be held in the refrigerator for a few hours by pressing plastic wrap against the surface of the salsa to prevent browning.*

Enchiladas del Suelo * PAGE 90

Pork *Carne de Cerdo*

Enchiladas de Aguascalientes

Yields 12 enchiladas / Serves 4

INGREDIENTS

For the sauce:

* ⅓ cup (79 ml) whole milk
* 3 ancho chiles (45 grams), cleaned, destemmed, deseeded, and dry roasted (see page 58)
* 5 tomatillos, husks removed and simmered in water until tender (approximately 10 minutes)
* 1 cup (120 grams) queso añejo, crumbled
* ½ cup (118 ml) crema Mexicana
* 2 tablespoons (30 grams) lard or vegetable oil

For the filling:

* 2 tablespoons (30 grams) lard or vegetable oil
* 9 ounces (255 grams) chorizo
* 2 cups (300 grams) Yukon Gold potatoes, peeled, medium dice, simmered until barely tender (5–7 minutes), and divided (1 cup, 150 grams, reserved for garnish)
* Kosher salt to taste

For the assembly:

* 12 corn tortillas
* Lard or vegetable oil as needed for softening tortillas

For the garnish:

* 1 cup (150 grams) reserved Yukon Gold potatoes, fried
* Shredded lettuce
* 1 cup (120 grams) queso añejo, crumbled

DIRECTIONS

Start with the sauce:

* Heat the milk in a saucepan over medium heat but do not boil. Turn off heat and add the ancho chiles and soak for about 10 minutes, or until tender. Place a spoon or other weight on the chiles to help keep them immersed in the milk.

* Drain, discard the milk, and place the chiles in a blender along with the tomatillos; add queso añejo and enough water to process. Blend until smooth. Stir in crema Mexicana.

* Heat the lard or oil in a saucepan over medium-high heat. Add the blended chile sauce to the saucepan and cook, stirring constantly, until it reaches a simmer. Reduce heat to low and continue cooking the sauce, stirring occasionally, for about 10 minutes, to allow the flavors to meld. Add a little water as needed to maintain a medium sauce consistency. Season with salt to taste, cover, set aside, and keep warm. Do not boil.

Prepare the filling:

* Place 2 tablespoons (30 grams) lard or oil in a heavy skillet over medium-high heat. Remove the casing and add the chorizo, breaking it up with a spoon. Continue stirring and sautéing until it is just cooked through.

* Add 1 cup (150 grams) potatoes. Continue to sauté, stirring occasionally, until the potatoes and chorizo are lightly browned. Season with salt to taste, cover, set aside, and keep warm.

Assemble the enchiladas:

* Add lard or oil to a depth of $^1/_2$ inch (12 mm) in a heavy skillet over medium-high heat. Heat to medium frying temperature, about 350°F (177°C).

* Fry the remaining potatoes in oil until golden. (They will be used for garnish.) Drain on paper towels, set aside, and keep warm.

* Reduce heat to low frying temperature, about 300°F (150°C).

* Place each tortilla in the oil and fry for a few seconds, just long enough to soften. Drain on paper towels.

* Working quickly, spread a spoonful of sauce on a tortilla.

* Place 2 tablespoons chorizo/potato filling on the lower third of a tortilla, roll, and place on an individual plate, 3 per serving, or on a warmed serving platter large enough to accommodate the enchiladas in a single layer.

* Repeat with the remaining tortillas.

* When the enchiladas are plated, cover with warm ancho chile/cream sauce.

* Garnish with queso añejo, lettuce, and fried potatoes.

Enchiladas del Suelo (Sinaloa Style Enchiladas)

Yields 12 enchiladas / Serves 4

This recipe illustrates the wonderful balance between vegetables and meat so often found in Mexican dishes.

INGREDIENTS

For the sauce:

* 3 ancho chiles (45 grams), cleaned, destemmed, deseeded, and dry roasted (see page 58)
* ¼ cup (35 grams) white onion, chopped
* 1 medium clove garlic, peeled and crushed
* 2 tablespoons (30 ml) vegetable oil
* 1 teaspoon (5 ml) white vinegar
* Sea salt to taste

For the filling:

* 10 ounces (283 grams) chorizo
* 6 green onions (about 25 grams), some green part included, thinly sliced
* 1 cup (200 grams) tomatoes, peeled, deseeded, and diced
* ¾ cup (90 grams) queso fresco, crumbled

For the assembly:

* 12 corn tortillas
* Vegetable oil as needed for softening tortillas

For the garnish:

* Avocado slices
* Lime juice, to sprinkle on avocados
* ¾ cup (178 ml) crema Mexicana
* 1 cucumber, peeled, seeded, and diced
* 6 radishes, sliced into rounds
* Shredded romaine lettuce
* ½ cup (60 grams) queso fresco, crumbled
* Cebolla Encurtida (see page 82)

Recommended accompaniment:

* Refried pinto beans (see page 63)

DIRECTIONS

Start with the sauce:

* Place the ancho chiles in a small pan over medium heat, cover with water, and simmer for 10–15 minutes, or until softened.

* Place the chiles, onion, and garlic in a blender and process to a purée, adding water as needed to achieve a medium sauce consistency. Pass through a medium-mesh strainer and set aside.

* Place 2 tablespoons (30 ml) vegetable oil in a saucepan over medium heat.

* When hot, add the chile purée and cook, stirring occasionally, until the sauce thickens slightly. Add vinegar and salt to taste. Add water as needed to attain a medium sauce consistency.

* Cover, set aside, and keep warm.

Prepare the filling:

* Place a heavy skillet over medium-high heat.

* When the skillet is hot, remove the casing from the chorizo and add it to the pan, breaking it up with a wooden spoon.

* Cook until crisply browned. Cover, set aside, and keep warm.

* Mix the green onion, tomatoes, and queso fresco together and set aside.

Assemble the enchiladas:

* Sprinkle avocado slices with lime juice to prevent browning.

* Have remaining garnishes ready and at hand.

* Pour oil to a depth of $1/2$ inch (12 mm) in a heavy skillet over medium-high heat. Heat to low frying temperature, about 300°F (150°C).

* Place each tortilla in the oil and fry for a few seconds, just long enough to soften. Drain on paper towels.

* Dip a softened tortilla in the warm sauce.

* Fill the lower half with 2 tablespoons chorizo and a generous amount of green onion, tomato, and cheese mixture. Fold in half and place on warm individual plate, 3 enchiladas per serving.

* When the enchiladas have been plated, garnish with crema Mexicana, cucumber, avocado slices, radish, cebolla encurtida, and queso fresco.

Enchorizadas

Yields 12 enchiladas / Serves 6

INGREDIENTS

For the tomato/chile de árbol sauce:

* 3 tablespoons (45 ml) vegetable oil, divided
* 1 pound (454 grams) chorizo, divided (half reserved for garnish)
* ³⁄₄ large white or yellow onion (105 grams), peeled and coarsely chopped
* 3 cloves garlic, peeled and crushed
* 6 dried chiles de árbol, destemmed
* 8 Roma tomatoes, quartered
* Kosher salt to taste

For the black bean sauce:

* 1 ¹⁄₂ cups (360 grams) cooked black beans (see page 60)
* Chicken stock as needed for puréeing beans
* 1 tablespoon (15 ml) vegetable oil
* Kosher salt to taste

For the filling:

* 1 small bunch cilantro, finely chopped
* ¹⁄₄ medium white or yellow onion, peeled, small dice, rinsed, and patted dry
* 1 ¹⁄₂ cups (180 grams) queso fresco, crumbled

For the assembly:

* 12 tortillas
* Vegetable oil as needed for softening tortillas

For the garnish:

* 3 hard cooked eggs, finely chopped or sieved
* ¹⁄₂ cup (60 grams) queso fresco, crumbled
* Reserved chorizo
* Avocado slices (optional)

DIRECTIONS

Start with the tomato/chile de árbol sauce:

* Place 1 tablespoon (15 ml) vegetable oil in sauté pan over medium-high heat.

* Remove casings and crumble the chorizo into a pan and sauté, stirring frequently, until golden brown. Remove it from pan and set aside. Reserve fat.
* Place 2 tablespoons (30 ml) oil in another sauté pan over medium-high heat.
* Add the onion and sauté for 2 minutes. Add the garlic and chiles de árbol and sauté for 1 minute. Add the tomatoes and cook until slightly soft and their juices have rendered. Cool slightly.
* Place the sautéed vegetables and half the sautéed chorizo in a blender and process until smooth. With the blender still running, add 1 tablespoon (15 ml) reserved chorizo fat and process until emulsified.
* Pour the sauce into a saucepan over medium heat and heat through.
* Add salt to taste, set aside, and keep warm.

Prepare the black bean sauce:
* Place the cooked beans in a blender with a little chicken stock and purée until smooth. Add more stock as needed to attain a medium sauce consistency.
* Heat 1 tablespoon (15 ml) oil in a large saucepan over medium heat.
* Add the black bean purée and cook, stirring frequently, until heated through.
* Add salt to taste. Cover, set aside, and keep warm.

Make the filling:
* Mix together cilantro, diced onion, and queso fresco.

Assemble the enchiladas:
* If using, have the recommended accompaniments ready and at hand.
* In a small skillet, gently warm the remaining chorizo for garnish, cover, and keep warm. Tomato/chile de árbol sauce should also be kept warm.
* Pour oil to a depth of 1/2 inch (12 mm) in a heavy skillet over medium-high heat. Heat to low frying temperature, about 300°F (150°C).
* Place each tortilla in oil and fry for a few seconds, just long enough to soften. Drain on paper towels.
* Spread 2 tablespoons bean purée on individual warmed serving plates.
* Spread a generous tablespoon sauce onto a softened tortilla. Place 2 tablespoons filling on the tortilla, fold in half, and place on top of the bean purée, 2 enchiladas per serving.
* Repeat with the remaining tortillas, then cover with warm sauce.
* Garnish with egg, queso fresco, and reserved chorizo. If using avocado slices, place them on top right before serving.

Notes: *For additional flavor, remaining rendered fat can be added to the oil before frying tortillas.*

To sieve hard cooked eggs: Roughly chop, then rub through a medium-mesh strainer with the back of a spoon.

Enchiladas de Nayarit

Yields 12 enchiladas / Serves 4

INGREDIENTS

For the sauce:

* 3 ancho chiles (45 grams), cleaned, destemmed, deseeded, dry roasted, and soaked in hot water (see page 58)
* 1 Roma tomato, dry roasted (see page 59)
* ½ small white onion, peeled and roughly chopped
* Pinch of dried thyme
* Pinch of nutmeg
* Pinch of ground canela (Mexican cinnamon)
* Pinch of ground cloves
* Pinch of ground coriander
* 1 ½ tablespoons (22 grams) lard or vegetable oil
* Pork cooking liquid or water for thinning sauce
* Kosher salt and black pepper to taste

For the filling:

* 1 tablespoon (15 grams) lard or vegetable oil
* ½ cup (113 grams) chorizo
* ½ cup (113 grams) cooked and shredded pork shoulder (see page 71), cooking liquid reserved for sauce
* 2 tablespoons (28 grams) green olives (such as manzanilla), chopped
* 2 tablespoons (28 grams) capers, chopped
* 1 jalapeño en escabeche (pickled), chopped
* ½ small white onion, peeled, small dice, rinsed and squeezed dry
* 1 teaspoon (1 gram) parsley, chopped
* ½ cup (60 grams) queso fresco
* Kosher salt and black pepper to taste

For the assembly:

* 12 white corn tortillas
* Lard or vegetable oil as needed for softening tortillas

For the garnish:

* Queso fresco, crumbled
* 1 tablespoon (14 grams) pitted green olives, sliced
* 2 ½ teaspoons (12 grams) capers, drained

DIRECTIONS

Start with the sauce:

* Place the prepared ancho chiles, dry roasted tomato, onion, thyme, nutmeg, canela, cloves, and coriander in a blender and process to a smooth purée, adding enough pork cooking liquid or water to attain a light sauce consistency.

* Strain through a medium-mesh strainer.

* Heat 1 $^1/_2$ tablespoons (22 grams) lard or oil in a skillet or sauté pan over medium heat. Add the strained sauce and cook until it darkens and thickens slightly, about 10 minutes. Add $^1/_2$ cup (118 ml) pork cooking liquid or water, and continue cooking, stirring occasionally, until the sauce is thick enough to coat the back of a spoon. Season to taste with salt and black pepper. Cover, set aside, and keep warm.

Prepare the filling:

* Heat 1 tablespoon (15 grams) lard or oil in a skillet over medium heat. Remove the chorizo from its casing and add to skillet. Sauté the sausage, breaking it up and stirring often, until it is cooked through and lightly browned.

* Add the shredded pork, olives, capers, and jalapeño. Cook for 1 or 2 minutes more, stirring occasionally.

* Remove the skillet from heat. Stir in the onion, parsley, and queso fresco. Taste and season with salt and black pepper.

* Cover, set aside, and keep warm.

Assemble the enchiladas:

* Have the garnishes ready and at hand.

* Add lard or oil to a depth of $^1/_2$ inch (12 mm) in a heavy skillet over medium-high heat. Heat to low frying temperature, about 300°F (150°C).

* Place each tortilla in the oil and fry for a few seconds, just long enough to soften. Drain on paper towels.

* Dip a softened tortilla in the warm sauce. Place 2 tablespoons chorizo/pork mixture on the lower third of a tortilla, roll, and place on a warm individual plate, 3 enchiladas per serving, or on a warm platter large enough to accommodate the enchiladas in a single layer.

* Repeat with the remaining tortillas.

* When the enchiladas are plated, top with the remaining sauce and garnish with queso fresco, olives, and capers.

Note: The filling improves in flavor if made a day ahead of serving and refrigerated. Gently rewarm before using.

Pipián Sauce

Yields 3.5 cups (830 ml)

INGREDIENTS

* 2 cloves garlic, unpeeled
* 1 cup (127 grams) raw pepitas (pumpkin seeds)
* ½ cup (72 grams) plus 1 tablespoon (9 grams) brown unhulled sesame seeds (1 tablespoon reserved for garnish)
* 12 ounces (340 grams) tomatillos, husks removed, cored, and quartered
* 5–6 serrano chiles, destemmed and sliced
* 1 poblano chile, fire roasted, peeled, destemmed, deseeded, and roughly chopped (see page 57)
* 1 small yellow or white onion, peeled and chopped
* Approximately 2 cups (473 ml) pork or chicken stock
* ¼ cup (59 ml) vegetable oil
* Parsley sprigs
* Kosher salt to taste

DIRECTIONS

* Place the garlic, pepitas, and sesame seeds in separate areas on a baking sheet and roast in a 350°F (177°C) oven for a few minutes, stirring occasionally, until the pepitas and sesame seeds barely begin to color. Remove the pepitas and sesame seeds from the pan and set aside, reserving 1 tablespoon (9 grams) sesame seeds for garnish.
* Roast garlic a few minutes longer, until a few brown spots appear. Cool and peel.
* Place the pepitas, sesame seeds, garlic, tomatillos, serranos, poblano, and onion in a blender along with pork or chicken stock. Purée, adding a little more stock or water as needed, to achieve a medium sauce consistency.
* Place the vegetable oil in a saucepan over medium heat. Add the puréed sauce and gently simmer, stirring often, until the foam subsides and the sauce slightly darkens, 30–45 minutes. Add additional water as needed to maintain a medium sauce consistency. Remove from heat.
* Place several parsley sprigs in the blender with some sauce. Purée and add back to the sauce (this gives it a nice color). Add salt to taste, cover, and keep warm.

Notes: *Pipián Sauce is used for pork, chicken, or duck enchiladas.*

It can be refrigerated for a week or frozen for up to one month.

Because of the pepitas and sesame seeds, this sauce will not be perfectly smooth. The longer it is cooked, however, the more homogenous it will become. For a smoother texture, purée the finished sauce just before serving.

Pipián and Pork Enchiladas

Yields 12 enchiladas / Serves 4–6

INGREDIENTS

For the filling:

* 2 pounds (907 grams) pork shoulder, simmered until fork-tender and shredded (see page 71), cooking liquid reserved for sauce

For the sauce:

* 1 recipe Pipián Sauce (see previous page)

For the assembly:

* 12 corn tortillas
* Vegetable oil as needed for softening tortillas

For the garnish:

* 1 tablespoon (9 grams) toasted brown unhulled sesame seeds (reserved from sauce recipe)
* Cilantro leaves

DIRECTIONS

Start with the filling and sauce:

* If the pork has been prepared ahead of time, moisten it with the reserved cooking liquid or water and gently reheat in a microwave or on the stovetop. Set aside and keep warm.
* If the sauce has been prepared ahead of time, gently reheat.

Assemble the enchiladas:

* Pour oil to a depth of $\frac{1}{2}$ inch (12 mm) in a heavy skillet over medium-high heat. Heat to low frying temperature, about 300°F (150°C).
* Place each tortilla in the oil and fry for a few seconds, just long enough to soften. Drain on paper towels.
* Dip a softened tortilla in the warm sauce. Place 2 tablespoons shredded pork on the lower third of a tortilla, roll, and place on a warm serving platter large enough to accommodate the enchiladas in a single layer. (Enchiladas may also be individually plated, 2–3 per serving.) Repeat with the remaining tortillas.
* When the enchiladas are plated, cover with remaining sauce.
* Garnish with sesame seeds and cilantro leaves.

Enchiladas Potosinas

Yields 12 enchiladas / Serves 4

This unique but traditional enchilada is reminiscent of an empanada in that the filling is sealed inside the ancho chile-infused tortilla dough.

INGREDIENTS

For the tortillas:

* 2 ancho chiles (30 grams), cleaned, destemmed, and deseeded
* 1 pound (454 grams) corn masa dough (see note)

For the filling:

* ½ cup (60 grams) queso Chihuahua, grated (or substitute white cheddar or Monterey Jack)
* ½ cup (60 grams) queso añejo or queso fresco, grated or crumbled
* ½ medium white onion, peeled and minced

For the finish:

* Lard or vegetable oil as needed for deep frying enchiladas

For the garnish:

* Queso añejo or queso fresco, grated
* 2 medium carrots, peeled, small dice, simmered until tender, 4–6 minutes
* 1 medium Yukon Gold potato, peeled, small dice, simmered until tender, 4–6 minutes
* ⅓ cup (43 grams) frozen green peas, blanched in boiling water for 1–2 minutes
* ½ cup (113 grams) chorizo, casing removed, crumbled, and sautéed over medium heat until brown, about 8 minutes
* Salsa Cruda (see page 85)
* Guacamole (see page 18)

DIRECTIONS

Start with the tortillas:

* Place the prepared chiles in a bowl and cover with hot water. Soak until softened, about 10 minutes. Drain and discard the soaking liquid.
* Place the softened chiles in a blender along with just enough fresh water to process, and purée until very smooth.
* Strain through a medium-mesh strainer.

* Thoroughly knead the purée into the masa until evenly distributed. (If the resulting dough is too sticky, add corn masa flour, 1 tablespoon at a time, until the dough is workable.)
* Cover with a damp cloth and set aside.

Prepare the filling:

* Mix the queso añejo, queso Chihuahua, and onion together and set aside.

Shape, cook, fill, and fold the tortillas:

* Heat a lightly greased comal or iron griddle over medium-high heat.
* Divide the chile/masa dough into 12 equal portions and roll into balls. Cover with a damp cloth or plastic wrap.
* Using a tortilla press, make the tortillas (see page 48) and place one or two at a time on the hot comal.
* After the tortillas have cooked for a few moments, place 1 spoonful of the cheese filling mixture on one half of the tortilla, leaving a ¼-inch (6 mm) edge. When the tortilla is cooked enough to hold together, fold it over the filling and gently press edges to seal. Continue cooking a few moments longer, turning once, so the tortilla cooks evenly and the cheese slightly softens. Cover with a dry cloth and set aside.

Finish the enchiladas:

* Preheat the oven to 140°F (60°C).
* Have the garnishes ready and at hand. The chorizo and vegetables should be warm.
* Add lard or oil to a depth of 2 inches (5 cm) in a deep saucepan and heat to a moderate frying temperature, about 325°F (163°C).
* In batches to avoid crowding, fry the enchiladas until heated through. Drain on paper towels, place on warm individual plates, 3 per serving, and keep warm in a very low oven while frying the remaining enchiladas.
* When the enchiladas are fried and plated, garnish with the chorizo, carrot and potatoes, peas, and queso añejo. Drizzle with salsa cruda.
* Serve guacamole on the side.

Notes: *Chiles are not dry roasted for this recipe in order to preserve their color.*

To make 1 pound (454 grams) chile/masa dough from dried masa, blend 1 ½ cups (210 grams) masa flour, 1 ¼ cups (296 ml) fresh water, and softened chiles (see page 53).

If using fresh masa, purée softened chiles with just enough water to process.

Enchiladas Regias

Yields 12 enchiladas / Serves 4

Regias means "regal," and these enchiladas live up to their name, with a rich filling of chorizo and shredded pork, enrobed with a fragrantly spiced ancho chile sauce, and garnished with olives, capers, onions, and cheese.

INGREDIENTS

For the sauce:

* 3 ancho chiles (45 grams), cleaned, destemmed, deseeded, and dry roasted (see page 58)
* ¼ medium white onion, peeled and roughly chopped
* 2 jalapeños en escabeche (pickled), halved
* 1 sprig thyme
* 1 sprig parsley
* Pinch of fresh nutmeg
* Pinch of ground coriander
* ¼ teaspoon ground canela (Mexican cinnamon)
* 2 whole black peppercorns
* Pork cooking liquid (about 1 ½ cups, 355 ml)
* 2 tablespoons (30 grams) lard or vegetable oil for frying
* Kosher salt to taste

For the filling:

* 2 tablespoons (30 grams) lard or vegetable oil
* 3 ounces (85 grams) chorizo
* 9 ounces (255 grams) pork shoulder, cooked and shredded (see page 71), cooking liquid reserved for the sauce

For the assembly:

* 12 corn tortillas
* Lard or vegetable oil as needed for softening tortillas

For the garnish:

* ½ medium white onion, peeled and thinly sliced
* ¼ cup (30 grams) queso fresco, crumbled
* ¼ cup (56 grams) pitted green olives
* ¼ cup (56 grams) capers, drained

DIRECTIONS

* Have the shredded pork and reserved cooking liquid at hand.

Start with the sauce:

* Place the prepared dry roasted ancho chiles in a bowl and cover with hot water. Soak until softened, about 10 minutes. Drain and discard the soaking liquid.

* Place the softened chiles in a blender along with the onion, jalapeños, thyme, parsley, nutmeg, coriander, canela, peppercorns, and enough pork cooking liquid or fresh water to process (about 1 1/2 cups, 355 ml). Blend until smooth and strain through a medium-mesh strainer.

* Place 2 tablespoons (30 grams) lard or oil in a saucepan over medium heat.

* Add the blended chile mixture and fry until the sauce darkens slightly.

* Thin the sauce as needed with additional pork cooking liquid or water to achieve a light sauce consistency.

* Season with salt to taste. Cover, set aside, and keep warm.

Prepare the filling:

* Place 2 tablespoons (30 grams) lard or oil in a heavy skillet over medium-high heat. Remove the casing and add the chorizo, breaking it up with a spoon. Continue stirring and sautéing until it is cooked through.

* Mix the shredded pork with the chorizo. Heat through, cover, and keep warm.

Assemble the enchiladas:

* Add lard or oil to a depth of 1/2 inch (12 mm) in a heavy skillet over medium-high heat. Heat to low frying temperature, about 300°F (150°C).

* Place each tortilla in the oil and fry for a few seconds, just long enough to soften. Drain on paper towels.

* Dip a softened tortilla in the warm sauce.

* Place 2 tablespoons chorizo/pork mixture on the bottom third of the tortilla, roll loosely, and place on a warm individual plate, 3 per serving, or on a warm platter large enough to accommodate the enchiladas in a single layer.

* When the enchiladas have been plated, cover with the remaining sauce and garnish with thinly sliced onion, queso fresco, olives, and capers.

Enchiladas Rioverdenses

Yields 12 enchiladas / Serves 4

In this recipe, chiles are mixed into the tortilla dough, making the enchiladas a beautiful brick red color. Homemade refried beans are best, but canned refried beans may be substituted if in a hurry.

INGREDIENTS

For the tortillas:

* 2 ancho chiles (30 grams), cleaned, destemmed, deseeded, and soaked in water to soften (see note)
* 1 pound (454 grams) corn masa dough

For the filling:

* 2 tablespoons (30 grams) lard or vegetable oil
* 8 ounces (227 grams) chorizo
* 1/2 medium white onion, peeled and chopped
* 1 large Yukon Gold potato, peeled, medium dice, and simmered until barely tender, 5–7 minutes
* 1 large carrot, peeled, medium dice, and simmered until barely tender, 5–7 minutes
* 1 cup (260 grams) refried pinto beans (see page 63)
* Kosher salt and pepper to taste

For the assembly:

* Lard or vegetable oil as needed for softening tortillas

For the garnish:

* 1/2 cup (118 ml) Roasted Tomato Salsa, room temperature (see page 80)
* 1/2 cup (100 grams) tomato, diced
* 1 avocado, peeled, pitted, and sliced
* 1/2 cup (60 grams) queso fresco, crumbled
* Sliced jalapeños en escabeche (pickled)

Recommended accompaniment:

* Pickled pigs feet or pork skin

DIRECTIONS

Start with the tortillas:

* Place the prepared ancho chiles in a blender with just enough water to process.

* Thoroughly knead the chile purée into masa dough. (If the resulting dough is too sticky, add corn masa flour, 1 tablespoon at a time, until the dough is workable.)

* Divide into 12 equal portions and make the tortillas (see page 53).

Prepare the filling:

* Place 2 tablespoons (30 grams) lard or oil in a heavy skillet over medium-high heat. Remove the casing and add the chorizo, breaking it up with a spoon. Continue stirring and sautéing until it is cooked through.

* Add the onion and sauté for 2 minutes.

* Add the potato and carrots and continue to sauté, stirring occasionally, until vegetables are lightly browned and fully tender. Season with salt and pepper to taste, cover, set aside, and keep warm.

* Warm the refried beans, cover, set aside, and keep warm.

Assemble the enchiladas:

* Have the garnishes ready and at hand.

* Add lard or oil to a depth of ¹/₂ inch (12 mm) in a heavy skillet over medium-high heat. Heat to low frying temperature, about 300°F (150°C).

* Place each tortilla in the oil and fry for a few seconds, just long enough to soften. Drain on paper towels.

* Spread 1 tablespoon refried beans on half of a softened tortilla, followed by 2 tablespoons chorizo/vegetable mixture. Fold in half and place, slightly overlapping, on a warm individual plate, 3 per serving.

* When the enchiladas have been plated, garnish with tomato, avocado, queso fresco, and jalapeños. Serve tomato salsa on the side along with (optional) pickled pigs feet or pork skin.

Notes: Chiles are not dry roasted for this recipe in order to preserve their color.

To make 1 pound (454 grams) chile/masa dough from dried masa, blend 1 ¹/₂ cups (210 grams) masa flour, 1 ¹/₄ cups (296 ml) fresh water, and softened chiles (see page 53).

If using fresh masa, purée the softened chiles with just enough water to process.

Enchiladas Tultecas

Yields 12 enchiladas / Serves 4

This version of enchiladas is served open-faced. In the north central area of Mexico some varieties of guajillo chiles are called cascabel, which means "rattle" in Spanish.

INGREDIENTS

For the tortillas:

* 3 cascabel (guajillo) chiles, peeled, seeded, and deveined
* Pinch of cumin seeds, toasted in a dry skillet until fragrant, then ground
* Pinch of kosher salt
* 1 pound (454 grams) corn masa dough (see note)

For the topping:

* 2 tablespoons (30 grams) lard or vegetable oil
* ½ cup (113 grams) chorizo
* ½ medium white onion, peeled, small dice
* 1 cup (150 grams) Yukon Gold potatoes, peeled, small dice, and simmered until barely tender, 3–5 minutes
* 1 cup (140 grams) carrots, peeled, small dice, and simmered until barely tender, 3–5 minutes

For the assembly:

* Vegetable oil as needed for softening tortillas
* 1 cup (120 grams) cotija cheese, crumbled

For the garnish:

* 1 cup (50 grams) shredded iceberg lettuce
* ½ cup (100 grams) Roma tomatoes, medium dice
* Cotija cheese, crumbled

Recommended accompaniment:

* Cecina (salted, air cured beef, see page 26)

DIRECTIONS

Start with the tortillas:

* Place the prepared chiles in a bowl and cover with hot water. Soak until softened, about 10 minutes. Drain and discard soaking liquid.

* Place the softened chiles in a blender along with the cumin. Add enough fresh water to process and a pinch of salt, and blend at medium speed until completely smooth.

* Strain through a medium-mesh strainer.

* Thoroughly knead the chile purée into the masa until evenly distributed. (If the resulting dough is too sticky, add corn masa flour, 1 tablespoon at a time, until the dough is workable.)

* Cover with a damp cloth and set aside to rest for a few minutes.

* Divide the dough into 12–15 equal pieces, shape into tortillas, and bake on a heated, unoiled comal (see page 53).

Prepare the topping:

* Place 2 tablespoons (30 grams) lard or oil in a heavy skillet over medium-high heat. Remove the casing and add the chorizo, breaking it up with a spoon. Continue stirring and sautéing until it is cooked through.

* Add the onion and sauté for 2 minutes.

* Add the potato and carrots and continue to sauté, stirring occasionally, until the vegetables are lightly browned.

Assemble the enchiladas:

* Pour oil to a depth of $1/2$ inch (12 mm) in a heavy skillet over medium-high heat. Heat to low frying temperature, about 300°F (150°C).

* Place each tortilla in oil and fry for a few seconds, just long enough to soften. Drain on paper towels.

* Arrange 3 tortillas open-faced on each warmed individual serving plate.

* Top each tortilla with 2 tablespoons chorizo/vegetable mixture, followed by a sprinkling of cotija cheese.

* Garnish with lettuce, tomatoes, and cojita cheese.

* Pan-seared cecina may be served on the side if desired.

Notes: Chiles are not dry roasted for this recipe in order to preserve their color.

To make 1 pound (454 grams) chile/masa dough from dried masa, blend 1 $1/2$ cups (210 grams) masa flour, 1 $1/4$ cups (296 ml) fresh water, and softened chiles (see page 53).

If using fresh masa, purée softened chiles with just enough water to process.

Enchiladas Verdes de Tlaxcala

Yields 12 enchiladas / Serves 4

INGREDIENTS

For the sauce:

* 1 pound (454 grams) tomatillos, husks removed, and cored
* 3 poblano chiles, fire roasted, peeled, deseeded, and deveined (see page 57)
* $\frac{1}{2}$ cup (118 ml) crema Mexicana
* 1 large egg
* Kosher salt to taste

For the filling:

* $\frac{1}{2}$ medium white onion, peeled, small dice
* $\frac{1}{2}$ cup (60 grams) queso añejo, crumbled
* $\frac{1}{4}$ cup (60 grams) cream cheese
* 8 ounces (227 grams) pork shoulder, cooked and shredded (see page 71)

For the assembly:

* 12 corn tortillas
* Vegetable oil as needed for frying

For the garnish:

* Sliced radishes

DIRECTIONS

Start with the sauce:

* Place the tomatillos in a saucepan and cover with lightly salted water. Bring to a boil, reduce heat to a simmer, and cook until tender, about 10 minutes (do not allow tomatillos to burst). Drain.

* Place the prepared poblano chiles, tomatillos, crema Mexicana, and egg in a blender. Process at medium speed until smooth.

* Strain the sauce into a saucepan, partially cover, and keep warm over very low heat. Do not allow the sauce to boil. Add salt to taste.

Prepare the filling:

* Mix together the onion and queso añejo.

* Bring the cream cheese to room temperature about a half hour before assembling the enchiladas.

* Gently warm the shredded pork.

Assemble the enchiladas:

* Place foil on the stove and backsplash to facilitate cleanup.

* Have the filling and garnish ingredients ready and at hand.

* Pour oil to a depth of ¼ inch (6 mm) in a heavy skillet over medium-high heat. Heat to low frying temperature, about 300°F (150°C).

* Dip each tortilla in the sauce, allowing the excess to drain back into the saucepan.

* Fry each sauced tortilla in the oil for a few seconds, just long enough to soften. Drain on paper towels.

* Fill the lower third of a tortilla with 1 teaspoon (5 grams) cream cheese, some pork, onion, and a sprinkle of queso añejo.

* Roll and place on a warm individual plate, 3 per serving, or on a warm platter large enough to accommodate the enchiladas in a single layer.

* Pour the remaining sauce over the enchiladas and garnish with radishes.

Enchiladas Zacatecanas

Yields 12 enchiladas / Serves 4

INGREDIENTS

For the sauce:

* 4 poblano chiles, fire roasted, peeled, deseeded, and deveined (see page 57)
* ⅔ cup (158 ml) crema Mexicana
* ⅓ cup (79 ml) whole milk
* 1 serrano chile, destemmed and roughly chopped (optional)
* 1 tablespoon plus 1 teaspoon (20 grams) lard or vegetable oil
* ⅔ cup (80 grams) queso fresco, crumbled
* Kosher salt to taste

For the filling:

* 9 ounces (255 grams) pork shoulder, cooked and shredded (see page 71)

For the assembly:

* 12 corn tortillas
* Lard or vegetable oil as needed for softening tortillas

For the garnish:

* Shredded lettuce
* ⅔ cup (80 grams) queso fresco, crumbled

DIRECTIONS

Start with the sauce:

* Place the prepared poblano chiles, crema Mexicana, milk, and serrano chile (if using) in a blender and process at medium speed until smooth.

* Heat 1 tablespoon plus 1 teaspoon (20 grams) lard or oil in a saucepan over medium heat. Add the poblano mixture and reduce heat to low, stirring constantly. Add queso fresco (it will not melt). Add salt to taste. When the sauce is hot, remove from heat, cover, and keep warm.

Assemble the enchiladas:

* Gently warm the shredded pork. Have the garnishes ready and at hand.

* Add lard or oil to a depth of $1/2$ inch (12 mm) in a heavy skillet over medium-high heat. Heat to low frying temperature, about 300°F (150°C).

* Place each tortilla in oil and fry for a few seconds, just long enough to soften. Drain on paper towels.

* Dip a softened tortilla in the sauce.

* Fill the lower third of a tortilla with 2 tablespoons shredded pork, roll, and place on a warm individual plate, 3 per serving, or on a warm serving platter large enough to accommodate the enchiladas in a single layer.

* Repeat with the remaining tortillas.

* When the enchiladas are plated, pour the sauce over top and garnish with lettuce and queso fresco.

Enchiladas de Frijoles y Chorizo

Yields 12 enchiladas / Serves 4

There is nothing better than the combination of frijoles y chorizo especially when enhanced by the deep, smoky heat of morita chipotles.

INGREDIENTS

For the sauce:
* 4 Roma tomatoes, cored
* 3 dried morita chiles (or to taste), destemmed (or substitute 3 chipotles en adobo)
* 3 ½ cups (840 grams) cooked black beans with cooking liquid (see page 60)
* ½ medium white onion, peeled and roughly chopped
* 1 small clove garlic, peeled
* 3 tablespoons (45 grams) lard or vegetable oil for frying
* Kosher salt to taste

For the filling:
* 10 ounces (283 grams) chorizo

For the assembly:
* 12 corn tortillas
* Lard or vegetable oil as needed for softening tortillas

For the garnish:
* 1 small white onion, peeled and sliced into thin rings
* 1 cup (120 grams) queso fresco, crumbled

DIRECTIONS

Start with the sauce:

* Place the tomatoes in a saucepan, cover with water, bring to a simmer, and cook until tomatoes barely burst open.

* Soak the moritas in hot water until softened. (If using canned chipotles en adobo, skip this step.)

* Place black beans in a food processor or a blender along with the tomatoes, moritas (or undrained chipotles en adobo), onion, and garlic.

* Blend until smooth, adding bean cooking liquid or water as needed to attain a medium sauce consistency.

* In a large skillet, heat 3 tablespoons (45 grams) lard or vegetable oil, add the puréed bean mixture, and fry, stirring occasionally, until heated through.

* Season with salt to taste. Cover and keep warm.

Prepare the filling:

* Remove the casing and crumble the chorizo in a skillet over medium-high heat. Sauté, stirring often, until lightly browned. Set aside and keep warm.

Assemble the enchiladas:

* Have the garnishes ready and at hand.

* Add lard or oil to a depth of ½ inch (12 mm) in a heavy skillet over medium-high heat. Heat to low frying temperature, about 300°F (150°C).

* Place each tortilla in the oil and fry for a few seconds, just long enough to soften. Drain on paper towels.

* Working quickly, spread 2 tablespoons bean sauce on a tortilla, sprinkle with 2 tablespoons chorizo, fold in half, and place on a warm individual plate, 3 enchiladas per serving.

* Pour the warm bean sauce on top. (If it has thickened, thin with some bean cooking liquid or water to maintain a medium sauce consistency.)

* Garnish with queso fresco and the onion rings.

Enchiladas Motuleñas

Yields 12 enchiladas / Serves 6

This enchilada recipe gets its name from the ancient Mayan city of Motul in the Yucatán. The famous dish Huevos Motuleños (Eggs Motul Style) originated there and was the inspiration for this enchilada recipe. Along with eggs, it features black beans and habaneros—common ingredients in dishes from the Yucatán.

INGREDIENTS

For the filling:

* 1 tablespoon (15 ml) vegetable oil
* ½ medium white onion, peeled, small dice
* 1 small clove garlic, peeled and minced
* ¼ teaspoon (½ gram) ground cumin
* 2 Roma tomatoes, small dice
* 1 ½ pounds (680 grams) cured cooked ham, small dice
* 2 large Yukon Gold potatoes, peeled, small dice, and simmered until tender, 4–6 minutes

For the sauce:

* 2 tablespoons (30 ml) vegetable oil for sautéing
* ½ medium white onion, peeled, small dice
* 1 habanero chile, minced
* 6 Roma tomatoes, small dice
* ¼ cup (35 grams) carrots, peeled, small dice
* ¼ cup (33 grams) peas
* Kosher salt to taste

For the assembly:

* 1 ½ cups (360 grams) cooked black beans with broth (see page 60)
* Kosher salt to taste
* 12 eggs (2 per serving)
* Vegetable oil as needed for softening tortillas
* 12 tortillas
* Pea sprouts (optional)

DIRECTIONS

Start with the filling:

* Place 1 tablespoon (15 ml) oil in a large sauté pan over medium heat.
* Add the onion and sauté until transparent, about 5 minutes.
* Add the garlic and cumin and sauté for 1 additional minute.
* Add the tomatoes and cook until tender, about 5 minutes.
* Add the ham and potatoes and cook until just heated through.
* Remove from heat, cover, and keep warm.

Prepare the sauce:

* Place 2 tablespoons (30 ml) oil in a large sauté pan over medium heat.
* Add the onion and sauté until transparent but not brown.
* Add the habanero and tomatoes and cook until tender.
* Add ½ cup (118 ml) water and cook to a sauce consistency.
* Add the carrots and peas and cook until tender.
* Add salt to taste. Cover and keep warm.

Assemble the enchiladas:

* Preheat the oven to 140°F (60°C). Place two oven racks about 4 inches (10 cm) apart in the middle third of oven.
* Place the black beans in a blender and add just enough water to process to a thick purée. Place in a small saucepan and heat through. Season with salt to taste, cover, and keep warm. The sauce and filling should be warm.
* Fry the eggs, 2 per serving, and hold in warm oven until needed.
* Pour oil to a depth of ½ inch (12 mm) in a heavy skillet over medium-high heat. Heat to low frying temperature, about 300°F (150°C).
* Place each tortilla in oil and fry for a few seconds, just long enough to soften. Drain on paper towels.
* Working quickly, spread 2 tablespoons bean purée on a warm individual serving plate.
* Place 2 tablespoons filling and 1 tablespoon sauce on the lower third of a softened tortilla, roll, and place, seam side down, on top of plated bean purée, 2 enchiladas per serving.
* Repeat with the remaining tortillas.
* When the enchiladas have been plated, generously top each serving with sauce and garnish with the fried eggs and (optional) pea sprouts.

Enchiladas de Barbacoa * PAGE 124

✴ ✴

Beef *Carne de Res*

✴ ✴

Enchiladas de Machaca (Dried Beef)

Yields 12 enchiladas / Serves 4

Machaca gets its name from the Spanish verb machacar, *which means to "pound" or "crush." The beef is braised, shredded, dried, and then pounded. This process tenderizes the meat, though it should retain a somewhat chewy texture.*

INGREDIENTS

For the filling:

* 2 pounds (907 grams) beef brisket or chuck, cut cross-grain into 1-inch (2.5 cm) strips
* 4 teaspoons (12 grams) kosher salt, or to taste
* 2 teaspoons (6 grams) ancho chile powder
* 1 scant teaspoon (3 grams) ground black pepper
* ½ teaspoon (1 gram) ground cumin
* 1 large bay leaf
* 1 clove garlic, peeled and minced
* 1 cup (200 grams) Roma tomatoes, cored, deseeded, and diced
* 1 ¼ cups (175 grams) yellow or white onion, diced
* ⅔ cup (93 grams) green bell pepper, destemmed, deseeded, and diced
* ⅔ cup (93 grams) red bell pepper, destemmed, deseeded, and diced
* Beef stock or water
* 1 recipe Pico de Gallo (see page 81)
* 2 tablespoons (30 grams) lard or vegetable oil

For the sauce:

* 16 ounces (454 grams) cooked pinto beans and their broth (see page 60)
* 2–3 dried chipotles, destemmed (or substitute chipotles en adobo)
* ¼ cup (60 grams) lard or vegetable oil
* Kosher salt to taste

For the assembly:

* 12 corn tortillas
* Vegetable oil as needed for softening tortillas

For the garnish:

* Queso fresco, crumbled
* Machaca
* Avocado slices

DIRECTIONS

Start with the filling:

* Place the meat, seasonings, garlic, tomatoes, onion, and green and red bell peppers in a large pot.

* Cover with beef stock or water and bring to a boil.

* Reduce heat to a simmer and cook until meat is fork-tender, 3–4 hours.

* Remove the meat from pot. When it is cool enough to handle, finely shred with two forks. (Save the cooking liquid for soup, stews, etc.)

* Scatter the shredded meat on a baking sheet, sprinkle with salt, and place in a 225°F (110°C) oven. Bake until it is dry but still pliable, 1–2 hours.

* Pound the meat to break the fibers and to tenderize it. (Meat should retain some chewiness.) Reserve some of the machaca for garnish.

* Place 2 tablespoons (30 grams) lard or vegetable oil in a large sauté pan over medium heat.

* Add the meat and pico de gallo and stir or toss until heated through.

* Taste and adjust the seasoning. Cover, set aside, and keep warm.

Prepare the sauce:

* Place the pinto beans with broth and chipotles in a blender and process to a smooth purée.

* Place ¼ cup (60 grams) lard or oil in a saucepan over medium heat.

* When hot, add bean/chile purée and cook until heated through. Add water, beef cooking liquid, or bean broth as needed to achieve a medium sauce consistency.

* Season with salt to taste. Cover, set aside, and keep warm.

Assemble the enchiladas:

* Pour oil to a depth of ½ inch (12 mm) in a heavy skillet over medium-high heat. Heat to low frying temperature, about 300°F (150°C).

* Place each tortilla in the oil and fry for a few seconds, just long enough to soften. Drain on paper towels.

* Place 2 tablespoons filling mixture on the lower third of a tortilla, roll, and place on a warm individual plate, 3 per serving, or on a warm platter large enough to accommodate the enchiladas in a single layer.

* When the enchiladas are plated, top generously with sauce.

* Garnish with queso fresco, machaca, and avocado slices.

Enchiladas Norteñas

Yields 12 enchiladas / Serves 4

INGREDIENTS

For the filling:

* 1 pasilla chile, destemmed, deveined, deseeded, and dry roasted (see page 58)
* ¼ cup (59 ml) vegetable oil, divided
* Kosher salt and ground black pepper to taste
* 1½ pounds (680 grams) skirt steak
* 1 medium white or yellow onion, peeled, medium dice
* 2 poblano chiles, destemmed, deseeded, medium dice (it is not necessary to fire roast for this recipe)
* 2 red bell peppers, destemmed, deseeded, medium dice

For the red jalapeño sauce:

* ½ cup (118 ml) vegetable oil
* 3 cloves garlic, peeled and crushed
* 1 medium white or yellow onion, peeled and sliced
* 10 red jalapeños, destemmed, deseeded, and deveined
* 2½ pounds (1.13 kilos) Roma tomatoes, cored and quartered
* 1½ tablespoons (14 grams) kosher salt, or to taste

For the assembly:

* 12 corn tortillas
* Vegetable oil as needed for softening tortillas

For the garnish:

* Queso fresco, crumbled

DIRECTIONS

Start with the filling:

* Place the prepared pasilla chile in a spice grinder and process to a powder.
* Lightly coat the steak with 1 tablespoon (15 ml) oil.
* Season with salt, black pepper, and ground pasilla chile to taste (see note).
* Grill the steak to medium-rare. Let it rest a few minutes and thinly slice. Cover and refrigerate until ready to assemble enchiladas.

* Place the remaining 3 tablespoons (45 ml) oil in a heavy skillet over medium-high heat.
* Add the onion, poblanos, and red bell pepper and sauté until vegetables are tender and beginning to brown.
* Season with salt to taste. Cover and set aside.

Prepare the sauce:

* Heat ½ cup (118 ml) oil in a large saucepan over medium-high heat.
* Add the garlic and sauté for 1 minute.
* Add the onion and sauté for 1 additional minute, or until the onion is translucent.
* Stir in the jalapeños and sauté for 1 additional minute.
* Layer the tomatoes on top of vegetables and cook until juices come out, about 5 minutes.
* Add ½ cup (118 ml) water, stir, bring to a boil, reduce heat to a simmer, and cook for about 10 minutes. Season with salt to taste. Cool slightly.
* Fill the blender half full with the vegetable mixture (in several batches) and process to a smooth purée, adding additional water as needed to attain a medium sauce consistency.
* Return the sauce to the pan and heat through. Taste and adjust seasoning. Cover, set aside, and keep warm.

Assemble the enchiladas:

* Return the skillet with the sautéed vegetables to medium heat.
* Add sliced skirt steak and toss or stir until the meat and vegetables are just warmed through (avoid overcooking). Cover, set aside, and keep warm.
* Pour oil to a depth of ½ inch (12 mm) in a heavy skillet over medium-high heat. Heat to low frying temperature, about 300°F (150°C).
* Place each tortilla in the oil and fry for a few seconds, just long enough to soften. Drain on paper towels.
* Spread 1 spoonful of sauce on a softened tortilla.
* Place 2 tablespoons steak/vegetable mixture on the lower third of a tortilla, roll, and place on a warm individual plate, 3 per serving, or on a warm casserole large enough to accommodate the enchiladas in a single layer.
* Repeat with the remaining tortillas.
* When the enchiladas have been plated, cover with sauce and queso fresco.

Note: *A good all-purpose meat seasoning is a 3:2:1 ratio of salt, ground black pepper, and ground pasilla chile.*

Enchiladas Placeras

Yields 12 enchiladas / Serves 4

INGREDIENTS

For the sauce:

* 1 pound (454 grams) Roma tomatoes
* 4 medium serrano chiles, or to taste
* 2 cloves garlic, peeled and coarsely chopped
* 3 tablespoons (45 ml) vegetable oil
* Kosher salt to taste

For the filling:

* 2 tablespoons (30 grams) lard or safflower oil
* ½ cup (70 grams) white onion, minced
* 2 cloves garlic, peeled and minced
* 1¼ pounds (567 grams) Roma tomatoes, cored, seeded, and finely chopped
* 1¼ pounds (567 grams) beef shoulder or chuck, cooked and shredded
* 1 cup (150 grams) sweet potato, peeled, medium dice, and cooked until tender in 1 cup (237 ml) beef cooking liquid (about 5 minutes)
* 4 chiles serranos en escabeche (pickled), or to taste, chopped
* 1¼ cups (296 ml) beef cooking liquid, divided (see page 71), some reserved for cooking sweet potato
* Sea salt to taste
* 3 rounded tablespoons (7 grams) cilantro, lightly chopped

For the assembly:

* 12 corn tortillas
* Lard or vegetable oil as needed for softening tortillas

For the garnish:

* ¼ cup (35 grams) white onion, minced
* ¼ cup (30 grams) queso añejo, grated

DIRECTIONS

Start with the sauce:

* Place tomatoes and serrano chiles in a saucepan over medium-high heat, cover with water, and bring to a boil. Reduce heat to a brisk simmer and cook until soft, about 5 minutes.

* Remove tomatoes and chiles from pan. Reserve 1 cup (237 ml) cooking liquid.

* Peel the tomatoes. Destem and coarsely chop the chiles.

* Place the garlic, cooked serrano chiles, and ⅓ cup (79 ml) tomato cooking liquid in a blender and pulse until roughly puréed, about 5 seconds.

* Add the cooked tomatoes and pulse for a few more seconds. Add additional cooking liquid as needed to achieve desired consistency (the sauce should retain some texture).

* Place 3 tablespoons (45 ml) oil in a frying pan over medium-high heat, add the sauce, and cook, stirring occasionally and scraping the bottom of the pan to prevent scorching, until slightly reduced (6–10 minutes).

* Season with salt to taste. Cover and keep warm.

Prepare the filling:

* In a heavy frying pan, heat 2 tablespoons (30 grams) lard or oil, add the onion and garlic, and gently sauté until the onion is translucent.

* Raise heat to medium-high, add tomatoes, and continue cooking, stirring and tossing the ingredients occasionally, until the mixture has reduced, about 10 minutes. Reduce heat to medium.

* Add the meat, sweet potatoes, serranos en escabeche, and ¼ cup (59 ml) beef cooking liquid.

* Add salt to taste, cover, and cook a few minutes longer. Stir in the cilantro. Remove from heat, cover, and keep warm.

Assemble the enchiladas:

* Add lard or oil to a depth of ½ inch (12 mm) in a heavy skillet over medium-high heat. Heat to low frying temperature, about 300°F (150°C).

* Place each tortilla in oil and fry for a few seconds, just long enough to soften. Drain on paper towels.

* Dip a softened tortilla in the sauce.

* Fill the lower third of a tortilla with 2 heaping tablespoons shredded beef mixture, roll, and place on a warm individual plate, 3 enchiladas per serving, or on a warm platter large enough to accommodate the enchiladas in a single layer. Repeat with the remaining tortillas.

* Cover with the sauce and garnish with onion and queso añejo.

Enchiladas de Ropa Vieja

Yields 12 enchiladas / Serves 4

Ropa vieja, *which means "old clothes" in Spanish, refers to the ragged and torn appearance of the meat.*

INGREDIENTS

For the filling and sauce:
* 2 pounds (907 grams) beef brisket or chuck, cut cross-grain into 1-inch (2.5 cm) strips
* 4 teaspoons (12 grams) kosher salt, or to taste
* 2 teaspoons (6 grams) ancho chile powder
* 1 scant teaspoon (3 grams) ground black pepper
* ½ teaspoon (1 gram) ground cumin
* 1 large bay leaf
* 1 clove garlic, peeled and minced
* 1 cup (200 grams) Roma tomatoes, cored, deseeded, and diced, divided
* 1¼ cups (175 grams) yellow or white onion, diced, divided
* ⅔ cup (93 grams) green bell pepper, destemmed, deseeded, and diced, divided
* ⅔ cup (93 grams) red bell pepper, destemmed, deseeded, and diced, divided
* Beef stock or water as needed

For the assembly:
* 12 corn tortillas
* Vegetable oil as needed for softening tortillas

For the garnish:
* Oaxaca cheese
* Avocado slices

Recommended accompaniment:
* Black Bean Rice (see page 68)

DIRECTIONS

Start with the filling and sauce:
* Place meat, seasonings, and garlic, along with half of the diced tomatoes, onion, and green and red bell peppers, in a large pot.

* Cover with beef stock or water and bring to a boil.
* Reduce heat to a simmer and cook until meat is fork-tender, 3–4 hours.
* Remove the meat from the pot, add the remaining diced vegetables, and increase heat to a brisk simmer.
* When the meat is cool enough to handle, shred with two forks or by hand, and sprinkle with cooking liquid. Cover and refrigerate until needed.
* Continue simmering the stock until it is reduced by about half.
* Remove the stock from the heat and allow to cool for a few minutes.
* Discard the bay leaf and transfer the stock and vegetables to a blender in multiple batches. (Be careful not to overfill the blender with hot liquids.)
* Purée the stock and vegetables, adding a little more water as needed to attain a medium sauce consistency.
* Transfer the sauce to a container, cover, and refrigerate, preferably overnight, to facilitate removal of fat.

Assemble the enchiladas:

* Remove fat from the surface of the sauce.
* Place in a saucepan and bring almost to a boil. Cover and keep warm.
* In a separate saucepan, mix the shredded meat with a little sauce and gently reheat. Cover and keep warm.
* Pour oil to a depth of ½ inch (12 mm) in a heavy skillet over medium-high heat. Heat to low frying temperature, about 300°F (150°C).
* Place each tortilla in oil and fry for a few seconds, just long enough to soften. Drain on paper towels.
* Spread 1 tablespoon sauce on a softened tortilla, followed by 2 tablespoons shredded beef. Roll and place on a warm individual plate, 3 per serving, or in a warm casserole large enough to accommodate the enchiladas in a single layer.
* Repeat with the remaining tortillas.
* When the enchiladas have been plated, cover with the sauce and garnish with Oaxaca cheese.
* Place under a broiler just long enough to melt the cheese, garnish with avocado slices, and serve with black bean rice if desired.

Enchiladas de Barbacoa

Yields 12 enchiladas / Serves 6

Barbacoa *traditionally refers to a cow's head placed in a pit lined with* maguey *(agave) leaves and hot mesquite coals, then slow cooked until the meat falls off the bone. Here, the tongue and cheeks (which many people consider the best parts) are used to create a barbacoa enchilada filling. The red jalapeño salsa, which is also the sauce for Enchiladas Norteñas, has just the right amount of heat and crisp acidity to balance the richness of the meat.*

INGREDIENTS

For the barbacoa:

* 1 beef tongue (about 2 ½ pounds, 1.13 kilos)
* 2 ½ pounds (1.13 kilos) beef cheeks, cleaned and trimmed
* ¼ cup (28 grams) garlic, minced
* ¼ cup (36 grams) kosher salt
* 5 bay leaves
* Hoja santa leaves or banana leaves for wrapping meat (optional)

For the sauce:

* 1 recipe Red Jalapeño Sauce (see page 118)

For the assembly:

* 1 recipe Cilantro Rice (see page 66)
* 12 corn tortillas
* Vegetable oil as needed for softening tortillas

For the garnish:

* 6 large, thin slices Oaxaca cheese
* 6 eggs
* Cooking spray or small amount of vegetable oil for frying eggs
* Cilantro sprigs or leaves

DIRECTIONS

Start with the barbacoa:

* Place the beef cheek meat on a perforated pan, cover, and refrigerate overnight to drain any excess blood.
* Mix the garlic and salt together in a bowl and generously rub into the tongue and cheeks.

* If using, place a large hoja santa leaf or banana leaf on heavy foil. Place the cheek meat on top and tightly wrap foil (or leaf and foil) around it, creating a packet.
* Create a second packet with the beef tongue.
* Place a few inches of water and bay leaves in a large stockpot or roasting pan.
* Place a steamer rack just above the surface of the water.
* Place the meat packets on the rack, cover, and cook over medium-high heat for about 1 hour. (Add water as needed to maintain the water level.)
* Reduce heat to a bare simmer and continue to cook for 8–10 more hours.
* When meat is fork-tender, remove from heat.
* When cool enough to handle, peel the skin from the tongue and trim the remaining fat or gristle from the tongue and cheeks. Shred the meat, cover, and refrigerate until needed.

Prepare the sauce:
* Prepare the red jalapeño sauce as directed (see page 118).
* If the sauce was prepared ahead of time, place in a saucepan over medium heat. When the sauce is heated through, reduce heat to low, cover, and keep warm.

Assemble the enchiladas:
* Preheat the oven to 325°F (163°C).
* Prepare the cilantro rice as directed (see page 66) and keep warm.
* The cilantro and cheese should be ready and at hand.
* Gently warm the shredded barbacoa.
* Warm 6 individual serving plates.
* Pour oil to a depth of $1/2$ inch (12 mm) in a heavy skillet over medium-high heat. Heat to low frying temperature, about 300°F (150°C).
* Place each tortilla in oil and fry for a few seconds, just long enough to soften. Drain on paper towels.
* Place a serving of rice on the center of an individual serving plate.
* Place 2 tablespoons barbacoa and 1 tablespoon sauce on the lower third of a softened tortilla, roll, and place, seam side down, on top of rice, 2 per serving.
* Repeat with the remaining tortillas.
* When the enchiladas have been plated, generously top each serving with the sauce and a slice of Oaxaca cheese.
* Place the plates in the oven long enough to heat the enchiladas through and melt the cheese.
* While the enchiladas are warming, fry the eggs, 1 per serving.
* When the enchiladas are ready, top each plate with an egg and cilantro.

Enchiladas Pachuqueñas * PAGE 134

Poultry *Pato y Pollo*

Mole Rojo

Yields 6–8 cups (1.5–2 liters) sauce

This is a good "do ahead" recipe, making the completion of Enchiladas de Mole Rojo easy.

INGREDIENTS

For the chicken and stock:
* 8 assorted chicken pieces, with bones and skin
* ½ large white onion, peeled
* 2 cloves garlic, peeled
* Kosher salt to taste

For the mole:
* ½ pound (227 grams) ancho chiles
* ¼ pound (113 grams) guajillo chiles
* 1 pound (454 grams) Roma tomatoes
* 1 large white onion, peeled and halved
* 8 medium cloves garlic, unpeeled
* 3 tablespoons (45 ml) vegetable oil, divided
* ⅔ cup (93 grams) pecans, chopped
* ⅔ cup (93 grams) unsalted peanuts
* 4 tablespoons (36 grams) brown unhulled sesame seeds
* 1 small stick Mexican canela (approximately 2 inches, 5 cm)
* 8 whole black peppercorns
* 4 whole cloves
* 1 tablespoon (1 gram) dried Oaxacan oregano or dried marjoram
* 1½ cups (355 ml) chicken stock
* 1½ ounces (40 grams) Mexican chocolate or less, to taste
* 1 tablespoon (9 grams) kosher salt, or to taste
* Pinch of sugar as needed

DIRECTIONS

Start with the chicken and stock:
* In a large stockpot bring 2½ quarts (2.33 liters) salted water to a boil.
* Add the onion half and garlic. When the water is vigorously boiling, add the chicken pieces and immediately reduce heat to a bare simmer.

* Skim any impurities and excess fat that rise to surface from time to time.

* Cook the chicken until fork-tender, 45 minutes to an hour.

* Remove the meat from stockpot. When cool enough to handle, shred meat, discarding bones and skin. Cover and refrigerate until needed for another recipe (may reserve 2 cups shredded meat for Enchiladas de Mole Rojo).

* Strain the broth, cover, and refrigerate until needed.

Prepare the mole:

* Remove the stems, seeds, and veins from chiles and dry roast them (see page 58).

* Transfer to a bowl of hot water and soak until softened, 15 minutes at most.

* While the chiles are soaking, dry roast the tomatoes, two onion halves, and unpeeled cloves garlic on an unoiled comal over medium-high heat (see page 59).

* There is no need to peel the tomatoes or onion after dry roasting. Peel garlic.

* Place 1 1/2 tablespoons (22 ml) oil in a skillet over medium heat and sauté the pecans and peanuts until golden.

* Add the sesame seeds, canela, peppercorns, and cloves, and stir until fragrant. Add the oregano and stir briefly. Immediately remove the nuts, seeds, spices, and herbs from the skillet to prevent overbrowning, and set aside.

* Transfer the softened chiles to a blender. Add enough fresh water to process to a smooth purée. Pass through a medium-mesh strainer.

* Heat the remaining 1 1/2 tablespoons (22 ml) oil in a large Dutch oven over medium-low heat. When the oil is hot, carefully pour the chile purée over the oil. Fry 5–10 minutes (a splatter screen helps with cleanup) until slightly reduced.

* Blend the sautéed nut/seed/spice mixture with the roasted tomatoes, onion, peeled garlic, and enough water to process to a smooth purée.

* Pass through a medium-mesh strainer, stir into the chile purée, and cook until the mole reduces by one-fourth.

* Remove any accumulated fat from the surface of the chicken stock and add 1 1/2 cups (355 ml) stock to the mole.

* When the mole is warmed through, taste and season with salt.

* Add the chocolate, a little at a time, until it tastes in balance with mole. (Amount will depend on the flavor intensity of the other ingredients. Also, depending on the bitterness of the chocolate, a pinch of sugar may be needed.)

* Let the mole simmer, stirring occasionally, until it coats the back of a spoon. Taste and adjust the seasoning before using.

Note: The mole may be refrigerated for up to 1 week or frozen for up to 1 month.

It is best to use true Mexican canela, which is much softer and easier to process than the hard stick cinnamon commonly sold in the United States (see page 42).

Enchiladas de Mole Rojo

Yields 12 enchiladas / Serves 4

Also called enmoladas, *which means "made with mole," this dish contrasts a simply prepared poached chicken with the complexity of a red mole.*

INGREDIENTS

For the sauce:

* 2 ½ cups (591 ml) Mole Rojo (see page 128)
* Water or chicken broth as needed

For the filling:

* 2 cups (260 grams) poached and shredded chicken (see page 70, or use chicken from Mole Rojo recipe)

For the assembly:

* 12 corn tortillas
* Vegetable oil as needed for softening tortillas

For the garnish:

* ⅓ cup (40 grams) queso fresco, crumbled
* 8 white onion rings
* 3 parsley sprigs

DIRECTIONS

Start with the sauce:

* Place the prepared mole in a saucepan over medium-low heat and add a little water or chicken broth as needed until slightly thin. Bring to a very low simmer for 5–10 minutes.

Prepare the filling:

* Place the shredded chicken in a saucepan over medium-low heat. Moisten with a little chicken broth or water and gently heat through.
* Cover, set aside, and keep warm.

Assemble the enchiladas:

* Pour oil to a depth of ½ inch (12 mm) in a heavy skillet over medium-high heat. Heat to low frying temperature, about 300°F (150°C).
* Place each tortilla in oil and fry for a few seconds, just long enough to soften. Drain on paper towels.

* Stuff the lower third of a tortilla with 2 tablespoons shredded chicken. Roll and place on a warm individual plate, 3 enchiladas per serving, or on a warmed serving platter large enough to accommodate the enchiladas in a single layer.

* Repeat with the remaining tortillas.

* When the enchiladas are plated, cover with mole, sprinkle queso fresco over the top, and garnish with onion rings and parsley sprigs.

Enchiladas Banderas

Yields 36 enchiladas / Serves 12

Banderas is the Spanish word for "flags," and Enchiladas Banderas is the perfect dish for special occasions such as Cinco de Mayo or Mexico's Independence Day, which is September 16.

Prepare 1 recipe Enchiladas Verdes de Pollo (see page 146), 1 recipe Enchiladas Suizas (see page 180 or 182), and 1 recipe Enchiladas Rojas de Queso (see page 174). Then place one of each enchilada side by side on individual serving plates to represent the colored stripes of the Mexican flag.

Enchiladas Divorciadas

Yields 24 enchiladas / Serves 12

The pairing of a green and a red enchilada is both colorful and delicious despite their "irreconcilable" differences.

Make 1 recipe Enchiladas Rojas de Queso (see page 174) and 1 recipe Enchiladas Verdes de Pollo (see page 146). Place one of each enchilada side by side on an individual serving plate. To maintain contrast, be careful to keep the sauces separated when topping the plated enchiladas. This is a great recipe for holiday entertaining or for large groups.

Enchiladas Huastecas con Pollo

Yields 12 enchiladas / Serves 4

La Huasteca is a cultural and geographical area along the Gulf of Mexico, which was home to the Huastec people before the Spanish conquest in the 16th century. The region includes parts of the states of Tamaulipas, Veracruz, Puebla, Hidalgo, San Luis Potosí, Querétaro, and Guanajuato.

INGREDIENTS

For the sauce:

* 1 pound (454 grams) tomatillos, husks removed, cored, and quartered
* 2–3 small serrano chiles, or to taste, destemmed and roughly chopped
* 3 small cloves garlic, peeled
* ¼ medium white onion, peeled and roughly chopped
* 3 cilantro sprigs
* 1 tablespoon (15 grams) lard or vegetable oil
* 1 cup (237 ml) chicken stock (preferably homemade)
* Kosher salt to taste

For the filling:

* 2 cups (260 grams) poached and shredded chicken breast (see page 70)

For the assembly:

* 12 corn tortillas
* Lard or vegetable oil as needed for softening tortillas

For the garnish:

* 1 cup (237 ml) crema Mexicana
* 1 cup (120 grams) queso añejo or queso fresco, crumbled
* Finely chopped white onion

DIRECTIONS

Start with the sauce:

* Place the tomatillos, chiles, garlic, roughly chopped onion, and cilantro sprigs in a blender and process at medium speed until smooth.

* Heat 1 tablespoon (15 grams) lard or oil in a saucepan over medium heat, add puréed tomatillo sauce, and cook until the color changes from bright green to yellow-green, 15 minutes.

* Add the chicken stock and cook until the sauce has slightly thickened, 15 more minutes.

* Season with salt to taste. Cover, set aside, and keep warm.

Assemble the enchiladas:

* Have the garnishes ready and at hand.

* Gently warm the shredded chicken breast for filling.

* Add lard or oil to a depth of $1/2$ inch (12 mm) in a heavy skillet over medium-high heat. Heat to low frying temperature, about 300°F (150°C).

* Place each tortilla in the oil and fry for a few seconds, just long enough to soften. Drain on paper towels.

* Dip a softened tortilla in the warm sauce.

* Place 2 tablespoons chicken on the lower third of a tortilla, roll, and place on a warm individual plate, 3 enchiladas per serving, or on a warm serving platter large enough to accommodate the enchiladas in a single layer.

* When the enchiladas are plated, cover with the remaining sauce and garnish with crema Mexicana, queso añejo or queso fresco, and onion.

__Notes:__ Add the serrano chiles a little at a time until the desired level of heat is attained.

A rotisserie chicken breast and low sodium canned chicken broth may be substituted for the chicken to save time.

Enchiladas Pachuqueñas

Yields 12 enchiladas / Serves 4

INGREDIENTS

For the filling:
* 2 cups (260 grams) poached and shredded chicken breast (see page 70)
* ¾ cup (90 grams) queso fresco, crumbled

For the sauce:
* 6 poblano chiles, fire roasted, peeled, seeded, and deveined (see page 57), divided (1 poblano reserved for garnish)
* 1 medium white onion, peeled and roughly chopped
* ½ cup (70 grams) roasted peanuts
* 1 slice French bread, soaked in 1 cup (237 ml) whole milk
* 1 tablespoon (15 ml) vegetable oil for frying
* ½ cup (118 ml) heavy cream
* Milk or water as needed for thinning sauce
* Kosher salt to taste

For the assembly:
* 12 corn tortillas
* Vegetable oil as needed for softening tortillas

For the garnish:
* Sliced radishes
* Shredded iceberg lettuce
* Reserved poblano chile, chopped
* ¼ cup (30 grams) queso fresco, crumbled

DIRECTIONS

Start with the filling:

* Mix the shredded chicken with queso fresco and set aside.

Prepare the sauce:

* Place 5 prepared poblanos (reserve 1 for garnish), the onion, roasted peanuts, and the bread with its soaking liquid in a blender and purée until smooth.

* Strain through a medium-mesh strainer.

* Heat 1 tablespoon (15 ml) oil in a saucepan over medium-high heat. Add the poblano purée, reduce heat to medium-low, and cook 5–8 minutes, or until sauce slightly darkens.

* Stir in the cream. Taste and season with salt. Gently simmer for a few minutes longer to allow the flavors to meld. Add milk or water as needed to attain a medium sauce consistency. Cover, set aside, and keep warm.

Assemble the enchiladas:

* Have the garnishes ready and at hand.

* Pour oil to a depth of ½ inch (12 mm) in a heavy skillet over medium-high heat. Heat to low frying temperature, about 300°F (150°C).

* Place each tortilla in oil and fry for a few seconds, just long enough to soften. Drain on paper towels.

* Dip a softened tortilla in the warm sauce.

* Place 2 tablespoons filling on each tortilla. Fold in half and place, slightly overlapping, on a warm individual plate, 3 enchiladas per serving.

* Garnish with radishes, lettuce, poblano, and queso fresco.

Note: If a spicier sauce is desired, one destemmed, chopped serrano can be processed with the chiles.

Pastel Azteca

Yields 1 casserole / Serves 6–8

Pastel Azteca, which translates to "Aztec cake," is composed of alternating layers of corn tortillas, tomato sauce, shredded chicken, chiles, cheese, and crema Mexicana placed in a casserole dish and baked.

INGREDIENTS

For the sauce:

* 2 pounds (907 grams) Roma tomatoes
* ½ medium white onion, peeled and roughly chopped
* 2 cloves garlic, peeled
* 2 tablespoons (30 ml) vegetable oil
* Kosher salt to taste

For the layers:

* 3 skinless, boneless chicken breast halves (each 8 ounces, 227 grams), poached and shredded (see page 70)
* 6 poblano chiles, fire roasted, peeled, destemmed, deseeded, deveined, and cut into strips (see page 57), divided (⅓ reserved for garnish)
* 1½ cups (355 ml) crema Mexicana
* 1½ firmly packed cups (180 grams) queso asadero, grated (or substitute Monterey Jack)

For the assembly:

* 12 corn tortillas
* Vegetable oil as needed for softening tortillas
* 1 tablespoon butter or vegetable oil for greasing casserole

For the garnish:

* Reserved poblano strips (rajas)
* Chopped tomato

DIRECTIONS

Start with the sauce:

* Place whole tomatoes in a saucepan, add $^3\!/_4$ cup (178 ml) water, cover with a lid, and cook over medium-low heat until the tomatoes barely burst open. Set aside to cool slightly.

* Transfer the tomatoes to a blender along with the onion and garlic. Blend until very smooth, adding the tomato cooking liquid as needed to achieve a thick sauce consistency.

* Heat 2 tablespoons (30 ml) oil in a saucepan, add the tomato purée, and cook until it slightly darkens, 10–15 minutes. Season with salt to taste, cover, and set aside.

Assemble the pastel:

* Preheat the oven to 350°F (177°C).

* Mix the shredded chicken with two-thirds of the poblano strips (reserve one-third for the garnish).

* Pour oil to a depth of $^1\!/_2$ inch (12 mm) in a heavy skillet over medium-high heat. Heat to low frying temperature, about 300°F (150°C).

* Place each tortilla in the oil and fry for a few seconds, just long enough to soften. Drain on paper towels.

* Butter or oil a shallow ovenproof casserole that will accommodate 4 tortillas in a single slightly overlapping layer (about $8\,^1\!/_2$ inches x 12 inches, 22 cm x 29 cm). The casserole should be suitable for serving.

* Spread a few tablespoons tomato sauce on the bottom of the casserole.

* Place 4 softened tortillas in a single layer on top of the tomato sauce, followed by half of the poblano/chicken mixture, a third of the remaining tomato sauce, $^1\!/_2$ cup (118 ml) crema Mexicana, and $^1\!/_2$ cup (60 grams) queso asadero.

* Layer with 4 more tortillas, the remaining chicken/poblano mixture, a third of the tomato sauce, $^1\!/_2$ cup (118 ml) crema Mexicana, and $^1\!/_2$ cup (60 grams) queso asadero.

* Top with the last 4 tortillas and the remaining tomato sauce, crema Mexicana, and queso asadero.

* Decorate the top with the reserved poblano strips.

* Bake in preheated oven until the cheese is melted and the pastel is heated through, 15–20 minutes.

* Remove from the oven and garnish with the chopped tomato. Loosely cover with aluminum foil and let rest for a few minutes before serving.

Enchiladas de Pato (Duck)

Yields 12 enchiladas / Serves 6

INGREDIENTS

For the duck confit:

* 2 tablespoons (18 grams) kosher salt
* Black pepper to taste
* 1 dried pasilla chile, ground in a coffee or spice grinder
* 3 duck leg quarters (each about 11 ounces, 312 grams)
* 4 cups (1 liter) duck fat, melted

For the sauce:

* ½ cup (118 ml) vegetable oil
* 2 cups (240 grams) yellow onion, small dice
* 6 dried morita chiles (chipotles), destemmed and deseeded
* 4 cloves garlic, peeled and quartered
* 1 ½ tablespoons (14 grams) kosher salt
* 2 pounds (907 grams) Roma tomatoes, quartered

For the filling:

* ¼ cup (60 grams) vegetable oil or duck fat (to cook filling)
* ½ cup (70 grams) yellow or white onion, small dice
* Prepared duck confit

For the assembly:

* 12 white corn tortillas
* Vegetable oil as needed for softening tortillas

For the garnish:

* 1 cup (120 grams) queso fresco, crumbled
* Minced cilantro
* Sliced radishes

DIRECTIONS

Start with the duck confit:

* Mix salt, black pepper, and pasilla together, and sprinkle over the duck legs.
* Place in a shallow baking dish large enough to hold the leg quarters in a single layer. Cover with plastic, and refrigerate for a minimum of 24 hours.

* Preheat the oven to 275°F (135°C). Remove leg quarters, clean and dry the baking dish, and rinse and pat the leg quarters dry. Return the duck to the dish and cover with melted duck fat.

* Place in the oven and bake until the meat is very tender (2 ½–3 hours). Allow to cool. Strain the duck fat through cheesecloth, shred the meat, and discard the bones.

Prepare the sauce:

* Place the oil in a saucepan over medium heat.

* When the oil reaches medium-low frying temperature, 325°F (163°C), add the onion, morita chiles, garlic, and salt.

* Cook, stirring constantly, until the onion is translucent, 3–5 minutes.

* Add the tomatoes and ½ cup (118 ml) water and raise heat to high.

* Once the mixture comes to a boil, lower heat and simmer for 5 minutes. Cool.

* Place the ingredients in a blender (in batches) and process to a smooth purée.

* Taste and adjust the seasoning. Return the sauce to the saucepan, heat, cover, and keep warm.

Make the filling:

* Place ¼ cup (60 grams) oil or duck fat in a sauté pan over medium heat.

* When the oil is hot, add the onion. Sauté until the onion is lightly browned.

* Add the cooked and shredded duck, reduce heat, and gently toss or stir until heated through. Cover, set aside, and keep warm.

Assemble the enchiladas:

* Pour oil to a depth of ½ inch (12 mm) in a heavy skillet over medium-high heat. Heat to low frying temperature, about 300°F (150°C).

* Place each tortilla in the oil and fry for a few seconds, just long enough to soften. Drain on paper towels.

* Place 2 tablespoons shredded duck mixture on the lower third of a softened tortilla, roll, and place on an individual plate, 2 per serving, or on a warmed platter large enough to accommodate the enchiladas in a single layer. Repeat with the remaining tortillas.

* When the enchiladas are plated, cover with morita sauce and garnish with queso fresco, radishes, and cilantro.

Note: If not using duck immediately after preparing, place the leg quarters in an ovenproof storage container and cover with duck fat. (Duck will keep several months under refrigeration if completely immersed in fat.) When ready to proceed, gently warm container with duck in a low oven. Remove duck and blot with paper towels. Shred meat by hand, discarding bones. Duck fat can be strained, frozen, and reused.

Enchiladas Queretanas

Yields 12 enchiladas / Serves 4

INGREDIENTS

For the sauce:

* 3 cups (710 ml) whole milk
* 2 ancho chiles (30 grams), cleaned, destemmed, deseeded, and dry roasted (see page 58)
* 1 small clove garlic, peeled
* Kosher salt to taste
* 1 large egg

For the filling:

* 1/3 cup (79 ml) vegetable oil for frying
* 1 large Yukon Gold potato, peeled, medium dice
* 2 large carrots, peeled, medium dice
* Kosher salt to taste
* 2 cups (260 grams) poached and shredded chicken breast (see page 70)

For the assembly:

* 12 white corn tortillas, preferably a few days old
* Vegetable oil as needed for frying

For the garnish:

* 1/2 cup (15 grams) romaine lettuce, shredded
* 1/3 cup (40 grams) queso fresco or queso ranchero, grated or crumbled
* 1/4 cup (8 grams) cilantro, chopped
* Crema Mexicana

DIRECTIONS

Start with the sauce:

* In a small saucepan, heat the milk to just below a boil and remove from heat.

* Add the prepared chiles and garlic and soak until chiles are soft, about 10 minutes.

* Transfer the chiles, milk, and garlic to a blender and process to a smooth purée. The sauce should be relatively thin (see note).

* Season with salt to taste. (Don't be afraid to aggressively season the sauce to make it stand up to the filling.)

* Add the egg and process for a few more seconds. Pour into a saucepan on medium heat, heat through, cover, and keep warm; do not let the sauce boil.

Prepare the filling:

* Heat ⅓ cup (79 ml) oil in a medium skillet over medium heat.

* Add the potatoes and fry until they begin to brown.

* Add the carrots and fry for an additional 2 minutes.

* Add salt to taste.

* Mix in the shredded chicken. Taste and adjust the seasoning.

* Cover, set aside, and keep warm (see note).

Assemble the enchiladas:

* Have garnishes ready and at hand.

* Place aluminum foil on the stovetop and backsplash to facilitate cleanup.

* Pour oil to a depth of ¼ inch (6 mm) in a heavy skillet over medium-high heat. Heat to medium frying temperature, about 300°F (150°C).

* Dip each tortilla in the warm sauce.

* Place in the oil and fry for a few seconds on each side. (Be careful. If the oil is too hot, it will splatter.)

* Place 2 tablespoons chicken/vegetable mixture on the lower third of a tortilla, roll, and place on a warm individual plate, 3 per serving, or on a warm serving platter large enough to accommodate the enchiladas in a single layer.

* Repeat with the remaining tortillas.

* When the enchiladas are plated, top with the remaining sauce and garnish with lettuce, cheese, cilantro, and a drizzle of crema Mexicana.

Note: If the sauce is too thick, it will not stick to the tortillas when frying.

Alternate version: Another version of Queretanas calls for only chicken and queso fresco to be used as the filling. The rolled enchiladas are placed on a bed of romaine lettuce and topped with fried, diced carrot and potato, as well as garnishes of cheese, cilantro, and crema Mexicana.

Enchiladas Rojas

Yields 12 enchiladas / Serves 4

INGREDIENTS

For the sauce:

* 4 guajillo chiles, cleaned, destemmed, deseeded, and dry roasted (see page 58)
* 2 pasilla chiles, cleaned, destemmed, deseeded, and dry roasted
* 3 Roma tomatoes (10 ounces, 283 grams)
* ¼ white onion, unpeeled
* 2 small cloves garlic, unpeeled
* 2 small sprigs marjoram
* 1½–2 cups (355–473 ml) chicken stock
* 1 tablespoon plus 1 teaspoon (20 ml) vegetable oil
* Kosher salt to taste

For the filling:

* 2 chicken breasts (each 8 ounces, 227 grams), bone in, skin on, poached and shredded (see page 70)

For the assembly:

* 12 corn tortillas
* Vegetable oil as needed for softening the tortillas

For the garnish:

* 1 white onion, peeled and thinly sliced
* 1 cup (120 grams) queso fresco, crumbled
* ½ cup (118 ml) crema Mexicana or crème fraiche (optional, see note)

DIRECTIONS

Start with the sauce:

* Soak the prepared guajillo and pasilla chiles in warm water until softened, but no more than 15 minutes.

* On an unoiled comal or iron griddle over medium-high heat, dry roast the tomatoes, onion, and garlic (see page 59). Core the tomatoes, discard the outer papery skin from the onion, and peel the garlic.

* Drain the chiles and discard the soaking water.

* Place the chiles, tomatoes, onion, garlic, and marjoram in a blender. Process to a smooth purée, adding enough chicken stock to attain a light sauce consistency. Strain the sauce through a medium-mesh strainer.

* Heat 1 tablespoon plus 1 teaspoon (20 ml) oil in a skillet over medium heat.

* Add the puréed sauce. When it boils, reduce heat to simmer, and cook for about 10 minutes to allow flavors to meld. Add salt to taste, cover, and keep warm.

Assemble the enchiladas:

* Gently warm the shredded chicken.

* Pour oil to a depth of $1/2$ inch (12 mm) in a heavy skillet over medium-high heat. Heat to low frying temperature, about 300°F (150°C).

* Place each tortilla in the oil and fry for a few seconds, just long enough to soften. Drain on paper towels.

* Dip a softened tortilla in the sauce.

* Place 2 tablespoons chicken on the lower third of a tortilla, roll, and place on a warm individual plate, 3 per serving, or on a warm casserole large enough to accommodate the enchiladas in a single layer.

* Pour the sauce over the top and garnish with sliced onion and queso fresco.

Note: *If adding optional crema Mexicana, make sure the edges of the enchiladas are covered with plenty of sauce to keep them soft. Top with crema Mexicana, place under a broiler just long enough for the crema to begin to brown, and garnish with the sliced onion and cheese just before serving.*

Enchiladas Tapatias

Yields 12 enchiladas / Serves 4

A Tapatío is someone from Guadalajara, the second most populous city in Mexico. According to authors Guadalupe Rivera and Marie-Pierre Colle, Frida Kahlo and Diego Rivera served a version of this traditional recipe at one of their many dinner parties in Mexico City during the 1940s.

The onion and garlic are sautéed separately from the chiles to add texture to the sauce.

INGREDIENTS

For the sauce:

* 10 ancho chiles (150 grams), cleaned, destemmed, deseeded, and dry roasted (see page 58)
* 2 tablespoons (30 ml) vegetable oil
* ½ large white onion, peeled and finely diced
* 2 small cloves garlic, peeled and minced
* Kosher salt to taste
* Pinch of sugar (optional)

For the filling:

* 2 chicken breasts (each 8 ounces, 227 grams), bone in and skin on, poached and shredded (see page 70)

For the assembly:

* 12 tortillas
* Vegetable oil as needed for softening tortillas

For the garnish:

* ½ cup (118 ml) crema Mexicana
* ½ pound (227 grams) queso añejo, crumbled

DIRECTIONS

Start with the sauce:

* Place the prepared chiles in a bowl and cover with hot water until softened, about 10 minutes.

* Drain the chiles and discard the soaking liquid.

* Place the chiles in a blender along with enough water to process (about 3 cups, 710 ml), and blend at medium speed until smooth.

* Strain the sauce through a medium-mesh strainer and set aside.

* Heat 2 tablespoons (30 ml) oil in a sauté pan over medium heat. Add the onion and cook until translucent but not brown, 3–5 minutes. Add the garlic and sauté for 1 additional minute.

* Add the chile purée to the saucepan. Cook about 10 minutes, stirring occasionally. Skim any oil that rises to the surface.

* Taste and season with salt and a pinch of sugar, if needed.

* Set aside and keep warm.

Assemble the enchiladas:

* The shredded chicken should be warm and at hand.

* Pour oil to a depth of ½ inch (12 mm) in a heavy skillet over medium-high heat. Heat to low frying temperature, about 300°F (150°C).

* Place each tortilla in oil and fry for a few seconds, just long enough to soften. Drain on paper towels.

* Fill the lower third of a tortilla with 2 tablespoons shredded chicken, roll, and place on a warm individual serving plate, 3 per serving, or on a warm serving platter large enough to accommodate the enchiladas in a single layer.

* When the enchiladas are plated, pour the remaining sauce over the top.

* Drizzle with crema Mexicana and garnish with queso añejo.

Enchiladas Verdes de Pollo

Yields 12 enchiladas / Serves 4

INGREDIENTS

For the sauce:
* 1 ½ pounds (680 grams) tomatillos, husks removed, cored
* 2 tablespoons (30 ml) vegetable oil
* ½ medium white onion, peeled and coarsely chopped
* 2 cloves garlic, peeled and minced
* 1 small serrano chile, destemmed and chopped
* ½ small bunch cilantro, chopped
* 1 tablespoon (9 grams) kosher salt, or to taste

For the filling:
* 3 cups (390 grams) poached and shredded chicken (see page 70)

For the assembly:
* 12 tortillas
* Vegetable oil as needed for softening tortillas

For the garnish:
* 1 ¾ cups (210 grams) queso asadero, grated (or substitute Monterey Jack)

Recommended accompaniment:
* Mexican White Rice (see page 66)

DIRECTIONS

Start with the sauce:

* Blanch the tomatillos in boiling water just until they change color and soften. Drain and set aside.

* Place 2 tablespoons (30 ml) oil in a large saucepan over medium heat.

* Add the onion and sauté until translucent, 3–5 minutes.

* Add the garlic and serrano chile and sauté for 1 additional minute.

* Put the onion mixture, tomatillos, and cilantro in a blender and purée.

* Pour the sauce back into the saucepan and bring to a simmer.

* Remove from heat and add salt to taste.

Assemble the enchiladas:

* The shredded chicken should be warm and at hand.

* Preheat the oven to 350°F (177°C).

* Pour oil to a depth of ½ inch (12 mm) in a heavy skillet over medium-high heat. Heat to low frying temperature, about 300°F (150°C).

* Place each tortilla in oil and fry for a few seconds, just long enough to soften. Drain on paper towels.

* Dip a softened tortilla in the sauce.

* Place ¼ cup (33 grams) shredded chicken on the lower third of a tortilla and roll closed.

* Place on an ovenproof individual plate, 3 per serving, or on an ovenproof platter large enough to accommodate the enchiladas in a single layer.

* When the enchiladas are plated, pour the sauce over the top, making sure the edges are well covered.

* Garnish with queso asadero.

* Place the enchiladas in the preheated oven just long enough to melt the cheese.

Enchiladas Callejeras

Yields 12 enchiladas / Serves 4

INGREDIENTS

For the sauce:

* 4 guajillo chiles or chiles de árbol, destemmed, deveined, deseeded, and dry roasted (see page 58)
* 10 ancho chiles, destemmed, deveined, deseeded, and dry roasted
* 1 medium white or yellow onion, peeled and coarsely chopped
* 4 cloves garlic, peeled
* 2 tablespoons (18 grams) kosher salt
* 1 cup (237 ml) olive oil

For the filling:

* 3 cups (390 grams) poached and shredded chicken (see page 70)

For the chorizo/vegetable topping:

* 8 ounces (227 grams) chorizo
* 1 large Yukon Gold potato, peeled, medium dice, and simmered until barely tender, 5–7 minutes
* 1 large carrot, peeled, medium dice, and simmered until barely tender, 5–7 minutes
* ½ cup (65 grams) frozen green peas, defrosted

For the assembly:

* 12 corn tortillas, preferably a day old

For the garnishes:

* Crema Mexicana
* Queso fresco
* Avocado slices
* Jalapeño en escabeche (pickled)

DIRECTIONS

Start with the sauce:

* Place chiles, onion, garlic, salt, and 4 cups (1 liter) hot water in a blender.

* Let sit for 5 minutes to soften chiles.

* Blend at medium speed into a smooth purée.

* With the blender running, add the olive oil in a slow steady stream and process until emulsified.

* Strain the sauce into a wide sauté pan over medium heat.

* Warm through, taste, and adjust seasoning. Cover and set aside.

Prepare the chorizo/vegetable topping:

* Remove the casing and crumble the chorizo into a large sauté pan over medium-high heat.

* Cook, stirring frequently to break up the chorizo, until it begins to brown, about 5 minutes.

* Add the potatoes and carrots and gently stir to combine. Cook, gently stirring occasionally, until the edges of the potatoes barely begin to brown.

* Remove from heat, stir in the peas, cover, and keep warm.

Assemble the enchiladas:

* Gently warm the shredded chicken. Have the topping and garnishes ready and at hand.

* Warm 4 individual serving plates.

* Heat a 9-inch (23 cm) nonstick sauté pan over medium-high heat. (The pan with sauce should be nearby.)

* Dip each tortilla in the sauce, making sure it's well coated, place in hot sauté pan, and quickly sear for about 3 seconds per side—just long enough for the sauce to begin to caramelize.

* Place 2 tablespoons shredded chicken on the tortilla, fold in half, and place on an individual serving plate.

* Wipe the sauté pan with a paper towel and reheat.

* Repeat the process with the remaining tortillas, slightly overlapping the enchiladas on serving plates, 3 per serving.

* When the enchiladas are plated, top with a drizzle of crema Mexicana, followed by a generous scoop of the chorizo/vegetable mixture and a sprinkle of queso fresco.

* Place the avocado slices and jalapeños en escabeche to the side of the enchiladas.

Open-Faced Shrimp Enchiladas * PAGE 160

Seafood *Mariscos*

Enchiladas de Atún (Tuna)

Yields 12 enchiladas / Serves 4

In the same way oil-packed, canned tuna is called for in a classic Niçoise salad recipe, it is also traditionally used in Enchiladas de Atún. However, finely diced, fresh tuna sautéed with the onions may be substituted if preferred.

INGREDIENTS

For the sauce:
* 5 Roma tomatoes (14 ounces, 400 grams)
* ½ medium white onion, unpeeled
* 2 cloves garlic, unpeeled
* 1 chipotle en adobo, or to taste
* ¾–1 cup (178–237 ml) bottled clam juice
* 1 teaspoon (5 ml) Worcestershire sauce
* Lime juice to taste
* Kosher salt and pepper to taste
* 2 tablespoons (30 ml) olive oil drained from cans of tuna (see note)

For the filling:
* 10 ounces (284 grams) canned tuna in olive oil (oil drained and reserved), divided (2 tablespoons for frying sauce and 2 tablespoons for frying filling, see note)
* ½ medium white onion (70 grams), peeled and minced
* 1 ½ tablespoons (13 grams) sesame seeds
* 2 tablespoons (30 ml) liquid from serranos en escabeche (pickled)
* 2 tablespoons (4 grams) cilantro, lightly chopped
* Kosher salt to taste
* 2 avocados
* Lime juice, to sprinkle on avocados

For the assembly:
* 12 tortillas
* Vegetable oil as needed for softening tortillas

For the garnish:
* Capers

DIRECTIONS

Start with the sauce:

* Dry roast the tomatoes, onion, and garlic on an unoiled comal or iron griddle over medium-high heat (see page 59). After dry roasting, core the tomatoes, discard the papery outer layer of onion skin, and peel the garlic.

* Place the tomatoes, onion, and garlic, along with the chipotle and $^3\!/_4$ cup (178 ml) clam juice, in a blender and purée.

* Add Worcestershire sauce and lime juice to taste, and pulse to combine. Add salt and pepper to taste.

* If the sauce is too thick, add additional clam juice as needed to attain a light sauce consistency.

* Heat 2 tablespoons (30 ml) oil drained from the canned tuna or vegetable oil in a saucepan over medium heat.

* Add the sauce and cook, stirring occasionally, until it reduces slightly. Taste and adjust seasoning.

* Cover, set aside, and keep warm.

Prepare the filling:

* Place 2 tablespoons (30 ml) oil drained from the canned tuna or vegetable oil in a sauté pan over medium heat.

* Add the onion and sesame seeds and cook until the onion is translucent and the sesame seeds are lightly browned, 3–5 minutes.

* Reduce heat to low. Add the canned tuna and juice from the serranos en escabeche and gently fold into other ingredients (avoid breaking up tuna too much).

* When the tuna is warmed through, gently fold in the cilantro.

* Season with salt to taste, cover, and keep warm.

* Slice the avocados (24 slices needed). Sprinkle liberally with lime juice. Cover and set aside.

Assemble the enchiladas:

* Pour oil to a depth of $^1\!/_2$ inch (12 mm) in a heavy skillet over medium-high heat. Heat to low frying temperature, about 300°F (150°C).

* Place each tortilla in oil and fry for a few seconds, just long enough to soften. Drain on paper towels.

* Dip a softened tortilla in the warm sauce.

* Place 2 tablespoons filling and 2 avocado slices on the lower third of a tortilla, roll, and place on a warm individual plate, 3 enchiladas per serving.

* When the enchiladas are plated, cover with the sauce. Garnish with capers.

__Note:__ If there is not enough oil from the drained cans of tuna to sauté the sauce and filling, make up the difference with vegetable or olive oil.

Enchiladas de Camarón (Shrimp)

Yields 12 enchiladas / Serves 4

INGREDIENTS

For the sauce:
* 1 recipe Chipotle Sauce (see page 191), divided ($1\frac{1}{2}$ cups, 355 ml, reserved for filling)

For the filling:
* 18 ounces (510 grams) medium shrimp (before peeling)
* Vegetable oil for sautéing
* $\frac{3}{4}$ cup (105 grams) white onion, minced
* Kosher salt to taste
* $1\frac{1}{2}$ cups (355 ml) reserved chipotle sauce
* 3 cups (360 grams) queso asadero, grated (or substitute Monterey Jack)

For the assembly:
* 12 tortillas
* Vegetable oil as needed for softening tortillas

For the garnish:
* 1 recipe Napa Slaw (see page 84)
* Crema Mexicana or sour cream
* Avocado slices (optional)
* 4 large grilled or sautéed shrimp, 1 per serving (if serving on individual plates)

DIRECTIONS

Start with the sauce:

* Prepare the chipotle sauce as directed (see page 191).

* If the sauce was prepared ahead of time, place it in a saucepan over medium-low heat, cover, and keep warm.

Prepare the filling:

* Peel, devein, and coarsely chop the shrimp. (Yield should be about 2 ½ cups, 400 grams, prepared shrimp.)

* Place a film of oil in a large heavy skillet over medium-high heat.

* Add the onion and sauté until translucent but not brown, 3–5 minutes.

* Add the shrimp and cook until opaque. (This should only take a couple of minutes.) Season with a generous pinch of salt, remove the shrimp from the pan, and set aside.

* Add 1 ½ cups (355 ml) chipotle sauce and the queso asadero to the sauté pan and stir gently until the cheese melts and the sauce slightly reduces, about 8 minutes. Taste and adjust the seasoning.

* Return shrimp to pan. Remove from heat, cover, and keep warm.

Assemble the enchiladas:

* Pour oil to a depth of ½ inch (12 mm) in a heavy skillet over medium-high heat. Heat to low frying temperature, about 300°F (150°C).

* Place each tortilla in the oil and fry for a few seconds, just long enough to soften. Drain on paper towels.

* Place approximately ¼ cup (30 grams) shrimp filling on the lower third of a tortilla, roll, and place on a warm serving dish large enough to accommodate the enchiladas in a single layer.

* Repeat with the remaining tortillas.

* Cover with the remaining chipotle sauce.

* Garnish with crema Mexicana, napa slaw, and (optional) avocado slices.

Optional plating method:

* For individual servings, place the napa slaw on a plate and top with the enchiladas (3 per serving) and chipotle sauce.

* Garnish with crema Mexicana or sour cream, (optional) avocado slices, and a grilled or sautéed shrimp.

Enchiladas de Camarón y Nopales
(Shrimp and Cactus)

Yields 12 enchiladas / Serves 4

INGREDIENTS

For the sauce:

* 1 recipe Chipotle Sauce (see page 191)

For the filling:

* 18 ounces (510 grams) medium shrimp (before peeling)
* Vegetable oil for sautéing
* ¾ cup (105 grams) white onion, small dice
* 12 ounces (340 grams) nopales, medium dice, rinsed and patted dry (see page 20)
* Kosher salt to taste

For the assembly:

* 12 tortillas
* Vegetable oil as needed for softening tortillas

For the garnish:

* 1½ cups (120 grams) Oaxaca cheese, shredded
* 1 recipe Napa Slaw (see page 84)
* Avocado slices

DIRECTIONS

Start with the sauce:

* Prepare the chipotle sauce as directed (see page 191).

* If the sauce was prepared ahead of time, place in a saucepan over medium-low heat and bring almost to a boil. Remove from heat, cover, and keep warm.

Prepare the filling:

* Peel, devein, and coarsely chop the shrimp. (Yield should be about 2 ½ cups, 400 grams, prepared shrimp.)

* Place a film of oil in a large heavy skillet over medium-high heat.

* Add the nopales and onion to the skillet and sauté until the juices released by the nopales have evaporated and the onion is translucent but not brown.

* Add the shrimp and cook until opaque. (This should only take a couple of minutes.) Add salt to taste. Remove from heat, cover, and keep warm.

Assemble the enchiladas:

* Preheat the broiler.

* Have the garnishes ready and at hand.

* Pour oil to a depth of ½ inch (12 mm) in a heavy skillet over medium-high heat. Heat to low frying temperature, about 300°F (150°C).

* Place each tortilla in the oil and fry for a few seconds, just long enough to soften. Drain on paper towels.

* Spread a little sauce on a softened tortilla.

* Place 2 tablespoons nopales/shrimp filling on the lower third of a tortilla, roll, and place on a warm serving dish large enough to accommodate the enchiladas in a single layer or on a warm individual plate, 3 per serving.

* Repeat with the remaining tortillas.

* When the enchiladas are plated, cover with chipotle sauce.

* Top with Oaxaca cheese and place under the broiler just long enough to melt the cheese.

* Garnish with the napa slaw and avocado slices.

Enchiladas de Playa

Yields 12 enchiladas / Serves 6

Enchiladas de playa (playa means "beach" in Spanish) are filled with sautéed black drum, shrimp, peppers, and onions, placed on a bed of white rice, topped with a roasted tomatillo/poblano sauce, and garnished with sour cream, Napa Slaw, and avocado slices.

INGREDIENTS

For the sauce:

* 2 pounds (907 grams) tomatillos, husks removed, cored, and halved
* ½ pound (227 grams) yellow or white onions, quartered
* ½ pound (227 grams) poblano chiles, destemmed, deseeded, deveined, and coarsely chopped (fire roasting is not necessary for this recipe)
* 4 ounces (113 grams) jalapeños, quartered
* Kosher salt to taste

For the filling:

* ¾ cup (178 ml) vegetable oil
* 1 ⅓ cups (187 grams) yellow or white onion, small dice
* ⅔ cup (93 grams) red bell pepper, small dice
* ⅔ cup (93 grams) poblano chile, small dice (fire roasting is not necessary for this recipe)
* 1 pound (454 grams) black drum, small dice (or substitute redfish, grouper, or red snapper)
* 1 pound (454 grams) medium shrimp (before peeling)
* Kosher salt to taste

For the assembly:

* 12 corn tortillas
* Vegetable oil as needed for softening tortillas
* Mexican White Rice (see page 66)

For the garnish:

* Crema Mexicana or sour cream
* 1 recipe Napa Slaw (see page 84)
* Avocado slices
* Lime juice, to sprinkle on avocado

DIRECTIONS

Start with the sauce:

* Mix the prepared tomatillos, onion, poblanos, and jalapeños together. Place in a vegetable grill pan and roast for 5–10 minutes over a hardwood or charcoal grill (fire should be mostly embers, not too smoky).

* Peel and discard any excessively blackened skin from the vegetables.

* Place the roasted ingredients in a blender and purée, adding water as necessary to attain a medium sauce consistency. Season with salt to taste.

* Pour the sauce into a saucepan over medium heat. When heated through, reduce heat to very low, cover, and keep warm.

Prepare the filling:

* Heat the oil in a sauté pan over medium heat.

* Add onion, red bell pepper, poblano chile, and a pinch of salt. Cook for 3–5 minutes, stirring frequently.

* Add the drum and shrimp and continue cooking until the seafood is opaque (about 3 more minutes). Add salt to taste. Cover, set aside, and keep warm.

Assemble the enchiladas:

* Sprinkle lime juice over the avocado slices, cover, and set aside.

* Pour oil to a depth of ¹⁄₂ inch (12 mm) in a heavy skillet over medium-high heat. Heat to low frying temperature, about 300°F (150°C).

* Place each tortilla in oil and fry for a few seconds, just long enough to soften. Drain on paper towels.

* For each serving, place ¹⁄₃ cup (55 grams) prepared white rice in the center of a warm plate.

* Working quickly, place 2 tablespoons filling on the lower third of a softened tortilla, roll, and place on the rice, 2 enchiladas per serving.

* Repeat with the remaining tortillas.

* When the enchiladas are plated, top with the roasted tomatillo poblano sauce.

* Drizzle with crema Mexicana or sour cream (a squeeze bottle works well for this) and garnish with napa slaw and avocado slices.

Open-Faced Shrimp Enchiladas

Yields 6 enchiladas / Serves 6

This is a good hot weather recipe, a great first course for summer brunches and light meals.

INGREDIENTS

For the vinaigrette:

* 5 guajillo chiles, cleaned, destemmed, deseeded, and dry roasted (see page 58)
* 2–3 chipotles en adobo
* Zest of 1 orange
* ¾ cup (178 ml) rice wine vinegar
* 1 tablespoon (10 grams) fresh ginger, peeled and grated
* 1½ teaspoons (1 gram) fresh oregano or ½ teaspoon (1 gram) dried Mexican oregano
* ½ teaspoon (1 gram) ground allspice
* ½ medium white onion, peeled, small dice, rinsed in a sieve, and patted dry
* 2 tablespoons (26 grams) sugar
* 1¼ cups (296 ml) vegetable oil
* Kosher salt to taste

For the shrimp:

* 24 medium shrimp (1¼–1½ pounds, 567–680 grams, before preparing)
* 2 tablespoons (30 ml) avocado oil or other vegetable oil
* Kosher salt to taste
* Guajillo chile powder to taste (see note)

For the assembly:

* 24 inner leaves from hearts of romaine lettuce, washed, dried, and torn into bite-size pieces
* 6 fresh white corn tortillas
* 12 cherry tomatoes, halved
* Cilantro microgreens (or substitute arugula, radish, or other spicy microgreens, see note)

DIRECTIONS

Start with the vinaigrette:

* Soak the prepared guajillo chiles in hot water until soft, about 15 minutes.

* Place in a blender along with the chipotles en adobo, orange zest, and vinegar, and pulse until the chiles and zest are finely minced.

* Add the ginger, oregano, allspice, onion, and sugar.

* With the blender running, slowly add the vegetable oil until emulsified.

* Add salt to taste. Whisk or shake well before using.

Prepare the shrimp:

* Peel and devein the shrimp.

* Place the avocado oil in large pan over medium-high heat.

* When the oil is hot, add shrimp and cook, frequently stirring or tossing, until just opaque, about 2 minutes. Be careful not to overcook.

* Remove the shrimp from pan. Season with salt and guajillo chile powder to taste, place on a warm plate, and loosely cover with foil.

Assemble the enchiladas:

* Have the salad components ready and at hand.

* Toss the romaine lettuce with just enough vinaigrette to coat.

* Warm the tortillas on a dry comal, iron griddle, or skillet until soft and pliable.

* Place the tortillas on individual serving plates, 1 per serving.

* Top with the dressed romaine lettuce and shrimp, 4 per serving.

* Garnish with the cherry tomatoes, 4 halves per plate, and microgreens to taste.

* Drizzle a little more vinaigrette over the top just before serving.

Note: *To make the ground guajillo chile powder: Clean, destem, deseed, and dry roast a guajillo chile until crisp and grind to a powder in a spice grinder.*

Microgreens are tiny vegetable greens that are harvested when a plant is very young—less than 2 weeks old and 2–3 inches in height. They add both flavor and visual interest to a dish.

Enchiladas de Jaiba (Crab)

Yields 12 enchiladas / Serves 6

Crab meat and a creamy poblano sauce are a luxurious combination and a good example of French culinary influence in Mexico.

INGREDIENTS

For the sauce:

* 2 tablespoons (28 grams) unsalted butter
* 1 cup (120 grams) shallots or white onion, thinly sliced
* 1 clove garlic, peeled and minced
* 4 poblano chiles, fire roasted, peeled, seeded, deveined, and cut into ¼-inch (6 mm) strips (see page 57), divided (¼ reserved for garnish)
* 2 cups (473 ml) crema Mexicana or crème fraiche
* Kosher salt to taste

For the filling:

* 2 tablespoons (28 grams) unsalted butter
* 1 cup (135 grams) fresh or frozen corn
* 12 ounces (340 grams) lump crab meat, picked over for bits of shell
* Kosher salt to taste
* Pinch of powdered chile de árbol, or to taste
* Lime juice to taste
* 2 green onions, thinly sliced

For the assembly:

* 12 tortillas
* Vegetable oil as needed for softening tortillas

For the garnish:

* Reserved poblano chile strips
* Mexican mint marigold leaves or fresh tarragon leaves (see page 43)

DIRECTIONS

Start with the sauce:

* Melt 2 tablespoons (28 grams) butter in a saucepan over medium heat.
* Add the shallot or onion and garlic and sauté gently until the onion is translucent but not brown, 3–5 minutes.
* Add three-quarters of the poblano strips (reserving remainder for garnish) and sauté for 1 additional minute.
* Transfer to a blender, add the crema Mexicana or crème fraiche, and process until smooth.
* Transfer to a saucepan over medium heat.
* After the sauce is warm, season with salt to taste.
* Add a little water as needed to attain a medium sauce consistency.
* Heat through, cover, and keep warm.

Prepare the filling:

* Melt 2 tablespoons (28 grams) butter in a nonstick skillet over high heat.
* Add the corn and constantly toss or stir until golden brown.
* Reduce heat to low. Add the crab meat and stir or toss for 1 minute.
* Add a generous pinch of salt and a pinch of chile de árbol (or to taste).
* Continue cooking, stirring constantly, until heated through.
* Add the lime juice to taste.
* Gently fold in the green onions.
* Taste and adjust the seasoning, cover, and keep warm.

Assemble the enchiladas:

* Turn on the broiler.
* Pour oil to a depth of $1/2$ inch (12 mm) in a heavy skillet over medium-high heat. Heat to low frying temperature, about 300°F (150°C).
* Place each tortilla in the oil and fry for a few seconds, just long enough to soften. Drain on paper towels.
* Dip a softened tortilla in the sauce.
* Place 2 tablespoons crab mixture on the lower third of a tortilla, roll, and place in an ovenproof casserole.
* When the enchiladas have been assembled, cover completely with the sauce.
* Place under a broiler just long enough to heat through. Garnish with the poblano strips and the Mexican mint marigold or tarragon leaves.

Enchiladas de Langosta (Lobster)

Yields 12 enchiladas / Serves 6

INGREDIENTS

For the sauce:

* 2 quarts (2 liters) heavy cream
* 2 cloves garlic, peeled and coarsely chopped
* 1 small white onion, peeled and coarsely chopped
* 6 poblano chiles, fire roasted, peeled, seeded, and deveined (see page 57)
* 1 small bunch cilantro
* ¼ cup (59 ml) crema Mexicana
* Kosher salt to taste

For the lobster:

* 2 medium white onions, peeled and quartered
* 6 ribs celery, halved
* 2 carrots, peeled and halved
* 7 ancho chiles, destemmed and deseeded
* 1 head garlic, halved
* 1 Mexican lager beer
* ¼ cup (59 ml) white vinegar
* ½ cup (72 grams) kosher salt
* 4 lobsters (approximately 1½ pounds, 680 grams each) or
  6 lobster tails (approximately 5 ounces, 140 grams each)

For the filling:

* 2 tablespoons (28 grams) unsalted butter
* 1½ cups (200 grams) fresh or frozen corn kernels, divided (½ cup, 68 grams, reserved for garnish)
* 3 poblano chiles, roasted, peeled, seeded, deveined, and cut into strips (see page 57)

For the assembly:

* 12 red corn tortillas (or substitute white or yellow tortillas, see note)
* Vegetable oil as needed for softening tortillas

For the garnish:

* ½ cup (68 grams) reserved sautéed corn kernels

DIRECTIONS

Start with the sauce:

* Place heavy cream, garlic, and onion in heavy saucepan over medium-high heat.

* Bring to a boil, reduce heat to medium, and simmer, stirring frequently to prevent scorching, until reduced by half. Cool for a few minutes.

* Place 6 prepared poblano chiles, cilantro, and crema Mexicana in blender.

* Add heavy cream mixture and process until smooth.

* Season with salt to taste.

* Strain and return to saucepan, cover, and keep warm, but do not boil.

Prepare the lobster:

* In a large stockpot, place 3 gallons (11 liters) water, onion, celery, carrots, ancho chiles, one-half head garlic, beer, vinegar, and salt. Bring to a boil and cook for approximately 10 minutes to develop the flavor.

* Fill a large bowl with equal parts ice and water for cooling the cooked lobsters.

* Add the lobsters to stockpot and cook for 10 minutes. (If using lobster tails, reduce cooking time to about 5 minutes.)

* Immediately remove the lobsters from pot and place in ice water to stop the cooking process.

* When cool, remove the meat from the shells and cut into bite-sized pieces.

Make the filling:

* Place the butter in a large sauté pan over medium-high heat.

* When hot, sauté the corn until golden. Reserve ½ cup (67 grams) for garnish.

* Add the poblano strips and lobster meat and stir until just heated through. (Do not overcook the lobster.) Remove from heat, cover, and keep warm.

Assemble the enchiladas:

* Have the sauce, filling, and garnish warm and at hand.

* Pour oil to a depth of ½ inch (12 mm) in a heavy skillet over medium-high heat. Heat to low frying temperature, about 300°F (150°C).

* Place each tortilla in oil and fry for a few seconds, just long enough to soften. Drain on paper towels.

* Place 2 tablespoons filling and a spoonful of sauce on the lower third of a tortilla, roll, and place on an individual plate, 2 per serving. Repeat with the remaining tortillas.

* When the enchiladas have been plated, cover with the sauce and garnish with a sprinkle of sautéed corn.

Note: *To make homemade red tortillas see page 53.*

Enchiladas Suizas, La Fonda on Main * PAGE 182

Dairy *Lácteos*

Enchiladas Huastecas con Huevos

Yields 12 enchiladas / Serves 4–6

This recipe, which includes cecina (air dried beef) and eggs, is delicious not only for the main meal of the day but also for breakfast or brunch.

INGREDIENTS

For the sauce:
* 1 ½ pounds (680 grams) Roma tomatoes, rinsed and chopped
* 3 serrano chiles (or to taste), stems removed and sliced
* 2 cloves garlic, peeled and minced
* 4 cilantro sprigs
* ¼ large white onion, peeled, small dice
* 1 tablespoon (15 grams) lard or vegetable oil
* ½ cup (118 ml) chicken broth
* Kosher salt to taste

For the filling:
* 8 large eggs

For the assembly:
* 12 corn tortillas
* Lard or vegetable oil as needed for softening tortillas
* Cecina (salted, air cured beef), thinly sliced (see page 26)

For the garnish:
* 1 cup (120 grams) queso fresco, crumbled
* ¼ large white onion, peeled, small dice
* Chopped tomato
* Fire roasted and chopped poblano chile (see page 57)

Optional topping:
* 4–6 fried eggs

DIRECTIONS

Start with the sauce:

* Place the tomatoes, chiles, garlic, cilantro sprigs, and onion in a blender and process at medium speed until smooth.

* Heat 1 tablespoon (15 grams) lard or oil in a saucepan over medium heat, add the puréed tomato sauce, and cook until it slightly darkens, about 10 minutes.

* Add the chicken broth and cook until it has slightly reduced, about 20 minutes.

* Season with salt to taste. Cover, set aside, and keep warm.

Prepare the filling:

* Break the eggs into a bowl, add a generous pinch of salt, and whisk well. Strain through a medium-mesh strainer (to remove any stray bits of shell) into a nonstick skillet over very low heat. Gently stir until the eggs form soft curds. Immediately remove from heat, place in a warm bowl, cover, and keep warm.

Assemble the enchiladas:

* Have individual serving plates ready and warm.

* Lightly grill or pan sauté 1 slice cecina per serving. Set aside and keep warm.

* Add lard or oil to a depth of 1/2 inch (12 mm) in a heavy skillet over medium-high heat. Heat to low frying temperature, about 300°F (150°C).

* Place each tortilla in oil and fry for a few seconds, just long enough to soften. Drain on paper towels.

* Place a piece of the cecina on a serving plate.

* Place 2 tablespoons warm scrambled eggs on a tortilla, fold in half, and place on top of cecina, overlapping the enchiladas slightly, 2–3 per serving.

* Cover with the sauce and garnish with queso fresco, onion, tomato, and poblano.

Optional topping:

* Place plated and garnished enchiladas in a very low oven while frying 1 egg per serving.

* Top each serving with a fried egg.

Papadzules

Yields 12 enchiladas / Serves 4

It is possible that a version of papadzules was made in pre-Columbian times, though the people of Mexico would not have had chicken eggs for the filling. Turkey, duck, wild bird, or even iguana eggs could have been used. There is no pork, beef, cheese, or fat for frying in this recipe—all of those ingredients were introduced to the Mexican people by the Spanish.

In the Mayan peninsula of Mexico, the pumpkin seeds used for this dish are much larger than those available in the United States. When ground in a molcajete and then squeezed, they exude oil which is drizzled over the enchiladas right before serving. If available, pumpkin oil can be used as a garnish. Chiltomate is a Mayan-inspired chile-tomato sauce.

INGREDIENTS

For the filling:

* 8 large eggs
* Kosher salt to taste

For the pepita sauce:

* 4 fresh epazote sprigs or 1 teaspoon (1 gram) dried epazote
* 1 cup plus 2 tablespoons (144 grams) raw pepitas (pumpkin seeds), divided (1 tablespoon, 10 grams, reserved for garnish)
* Kosher salt to taste

For the chiltomate sauce:

* 1 pound (454 grams) Roma tomatoes
* 1 habanero chile, whole
* ¼ medium white onion, peeled and root end removed
* Kosher salt to taste

For the assembly:

* 12 corn tortillas

For the garnish:

* 1 tablespoon (10 grams) reserved roasted pepitas
* Pumpkin oil (optional)

DIRECTIONS

Start with the filling:

* Place the eggs in a large saucepan that can accommodate them without crowding. Cover with cold water and bring to a boil over medium-high heat.

* Reduce heat to a bare simmer and cook for 7 minutes (yolks should be fully set yet tender). Immediately drain eggs and immerse in cold water to stop the cooking process. Peel and coarsely chop. Season with salt to taste and set aside.

Prepare the pepita sauce:

* Place 2 cups (473 ml) water in a saucepan over high heat. Add the epazote (if using dried, tie in a cheesecloth for easy removal) and bring to a boil. Remove from heat, steep for a few minutes, and discard epazote. Set water aside to cool.

* Place pepitas on a skillet set over medium-low heat. Dry roast until slightly golden, being careful to not let them burn. Remove from pan and allow to cool briefly. Set aside 1 tablespoon (10 grams) seeds for garnish.

* Grind the remaining seeds to a very fine powder in a spice grinder.

* Place ground pepitas in a blender with 1 cup (237 ml) water infused with epazote; purée, adding more epazote-infused water as needed to achieve a very smooth sauce consistency.

* Place the puréed pepitas in a saucepan over medium-low heat. Warm through but do not allow to boil.

* Season with salt to taste. Cover and keep warm.

Make the chiltomate sauce:

* Place the tomatoes in a saucepan, cover with water, and bring to a boil. Reduce heat to a brisk simmer and cook for 10 minutes.

* While tomatoes are simmering, dry roast habanero chile until browned in spots (see page 57).

* Place the tomatoes and onion in a blender and process until smooth, adding tomato cooking water as needed to achieve smooth consistency.

* Transfer the blended ingredients to a saucepan placed over medium heat.

* Add the roasted habanero chile (whole) to sauce and simmer gently for 10 minutes, or until the sauce is slightly reduced and flavored with the habanero. Remove the chile and discard.

* Season with salt to taste. Cover and keep warm.

Assemble the enchiladas:

* Place a tortilla in the warm pepita sauce, turning to cover completely with sauce.

* Place 2 tablespoons chopped egg on the lower third of a tortilla, roll, and place on a warm individual plate, 3 enchiladas per serving.

* When the enchiladas are plated, pour remaining pepita sauce over enchiladas (papadzules should be moist and well covered with this sauce).

* Top with chiltomate sauce and garnish with reserved pepitas and (optional) pumpkin oil.

Enchiladas de Requesón y Aguacate
(Soft Cheese and Avocado)

Yields 12 enchiladas / Serves 4

Requesón is a very soft whole milk cows' cheese that is somewhat similar to a mild ricotta. This is a very simple, light version of enchiladas—perfect for a hot summer day.

INGREDIENTS

For the sauce:

* 1–2 morita chiles, destemmed, deseeded, and deveined (or substitute 2 chipotles en adobo)
* 5 Roma tomatoes, dry roasted
* 1 large clove garlic, dry roasted (see page 59)
* 1 fresh epazote sprig or 2 cilantro sprigs
* 2 tablespoons (30 ml) vegetable oil
* Kosher salt to taste

For the filling:

* 1 1/2 cups (340 grams) requesón, ricotta, or very soft farmer's cheese
* 2 tablespoons (20 grams) white onion, chopped
* 1 tablespoon (1 gram) fresh epazote or 2 tablespoons (4 grams) cilantro, chopped
* Kosher salt to taste
* 2 large avocados (2 slices per enchilada, plus additional for garnish)

For the assembly:

* 12 corn tortillas
* Vegetable oil as needed for softening tortillas

For the garnish:

* Avocado slices
* Cilantro sprigs

DIRECTIONS

Start with the sauce:

* Place the morita chiles in hot water until softened, about 10 minutes (if using chipotles en adobo, skip this step).

* Dry roast the tomatoes and garlic on an unoiled comal or iron griddle over medium-high heat. Core the tomatoes and peel the garlic after roasting.

* Place the chiles, dry roasted tomatoes and garlic, and the epazote or cilantro sprigs in a blender and process until smooth, adding water as needed to attain a medium sauce consistency.

* Strain the sauce through a medium-mesh strainer.

* Heat 2 tablespoons (30 ml) oil in a saucepan. Simmer the sauce for a few minutes to develop flavor. Remove from heat and season with salt to taste. Cover, set aside, and keep warm.

Prepare the filling:

* Mix the requesón or ricotta cheese with the onion and chopped epazote or cilantro. Season with salt to taste.

* Slice the avocados (24 slices for filling, plus additional for garnish).

Assemble the enchiladas:

* Pour oil to a depth of ¹/₂ inch (12 mm) in a heavy skillet over medium-high heat. Heat to low frying temperature, about 300°F (150°C).

* Place each tortilla in the oil and fry for a few seconds, just long enough to soften. Drain on paper towels.

* Stuff each tortilla with some of the cheese mixture and 2 avocado slices.

* Roll and place on a warm individual plate, 3 enchiladas per serving, or on a warm platter large enough to accommodate the enchiladas in a single layer.

* Cover the enchiladas with sauce.

* Garnish with avocado slices and cilantro sprigs.

Enchiladas Rojas de Queso

Yields 12 enchiladas / Serves 4

INGREDIENTS

For the sauce:

* 1 recipe Chipotle Sauce (see page 191), divided (1 ½ cups, 355 ml, reserved for filling)

For the filling:

* 3 cups (360 grams) queso asadero, grated (or substitute Monterey Jack)
* 1 ½ cups (355 ml) reserved chipotle sauce

For the assembly:

* 12 red corn tortillas (see page 53)
* Vegetable oil as needed for softening tortillas

For the garnish:

* 1 cup (120 grams) queso fresco, crumbled

DIRECTIONS

Start with the sauce:

* Prepare the chipotle sauce as directed (see page 191).
* If the sauce was prepared ahead of time, place in a saucepan over medium heat. When sauce is heated through, reduce heat to low, cover, and keep warm.

Assemble the enchiladas:

* Have the cheeses for the filling and the garnish ready and at hand.
* Pour oil to a depth of ½ inch (12 mm) in a heavy skillet over medium-high heat. Heat to low frying temperature, about 300°F (150°C).
* Place each tortilla in the oil and fry for a few seconds, just long enough to soften. Drain on paper towels.
* Place ¼ cup (30 grams) queso asadero topped with 2 tablespoons chipotle sauce on the lower third of a softened tortilla.
* Roll and place on an individual ovenproof plate, 3 enchiladas per serving, or on an ovenproof dish large enough to accommodate the enchiladas in a single layer. Repeat with the other tortillas.
* When the enchiladas are plated, pour the remaining chipotle sauce over the enchiladas, being careful to fully cover the edges. Place under a broiler just long enough to melt the cheese.
* Garnish with queso fresco.

Enchiladas San Blas

Yields 12 enchiladas / Serves 4

This is a very simple open-faced enchilada recipe that gets its unique flavor from frying instead of toasting the dried chiles.

INGREDIENTS

For the sauce:

* 2 mulato chiles, cleaned, destemmed, deveined, and deseeded
* 2 ancho chiles, cleaned, destemmed, deveined, and deseeded
* $1/2$ cup (110 grams) lard or vegetable oil
* Approximately 4 cups (1 liter) whole milk
* $1/2$ cup (60 grams) queso fresco, crumbled
* Kosher salt to taste

For the assembly:

* 12 corn tortillas

For the garnish:

* Queso fresco, crumbled

DIRECTIONS

Start with the sauce:

* Heat the lard or oil in a sauté pan over medium heat. Add the chiles and fry briefly on both sides until softened.
* Remove the chiles from the oil, blot with paper towels, and place in a blender.
* Add 3 cups (710 ml) milk, and purée on medium speed until smooth.
* Strain the sauce into a pan over low heat. Add queso fresco, stirring constantly.
* When the sauce is warm, add just enough remaining milk to attain a medium sauce consistency. Season with salt to taste. Cover, set aside, and keep warm.

Assemble the enchiladas:

* Place a pool of sauce on each of 4 warm individual serving plates.
* Coat each tortilla generously with the remaining sauce, fold in half, and place slightly overlapping on the plates, 3 per serving.
* Garnish with queso fresco.

Notes: Many chefs reuse lard or oil used for frying chiles, because it is infused with chile flavor.

To make homemade red tortillas see page 53.

Enchiladas de Pulque

Yields 12 enchiladas / Serves 4

Pulque is a traditional Mexican fermented beverage made from the sap of various species of agave, or maguey. It is milky, slightly viscous, and foamy with a somewhat sour, yeasty taste. Mexican dark beer is an acceptable substitute.

INGREDIENTS

For the sauce:

* 2 ancho chiles, cleaned, destemmed, deseeded, and dry roasted (see page 58)
* 1 mulato chile, cleaned, destemmed, deseeded, and dry roasted
* 1 pasilla chile, cleaned, destemmed, deseeded, and dry roasted
* ½ medium white onion, dry roasted (see page 59)
* 2 cloves garlic, dry roasted
* 5 Roma tomatoes, dry roasted
* 1 whole clove
* ½ cup (60 grams) queso fresco, crumbled
* ¼ cup (59 ml) crema Mexicana
* Black pepper to taste
* ⅓ cup (79 ml) vegetable oil
* ¾ cup (178 ml) pulque or a dark beer such as Negro Modelo
* Pinch of baking soda
* Kosher salt to taste
* Sugar to taste

For the filling:

* 1 cup (120 grams) queso fresco, crumbled
* ¼ cup (35 grams) onion, minced

For the assembly:

* 12 corn tortillas
* Vegetable oil as needed for softening tortillas

For the garnish:

* ½ cup (60 grams) queso fresco, crumbled
* ¼ medium white onion, peeled and minced
* Shredded iceberg lettuce
* Sliced radishes

DIRECTIONS

Start with the sauce:

* Place the prepared ancho, mulato, and pasilla chiles in a bowl and cover with hot water. Soak until soft, about 10 minutes.

* Dry roast the onion, tomatoes, and garlic on an unoiled comal or iron griddle set over medium-high heat. Peel the garlic after roasting.

* Drain the chiles and discard the soaking liquid. Place in a blender along with the dry roasted onion, tomatoes, and garlic, and the clove, queso fresco, crema Mexicana, and black pepper.

* Add enough water to process and blend until smooth. Strain the sauce through a medium-mesh strainer.

* Heat $1/3$ cup (79 ml) oil in a medium Dutch oven over medium-low heat and add the sauce. Cook, stirring occasionally, until it thickens slightly.

* Stir in the baking soda and pulque or beer. Continue simmering until the sauce reduces to a medium consistency.

* Season with salt and sugar to taste. Cover, set aside, and keep warm.

Assemble the enchiladas:

* Have the filling and garnish ingredients ready and at hand.

* Pour oil to a depth of $1/2$ inch (12 mm) in a heavy skillet over medium-high heat. Heat to low frying temperature, about 300°F (150°C).

* Place each tortilla in the oil and fry for a few seconds, just long enough to soften. Drain on paper towels.

* Dip a softened tortilla in the sauce.

* Place 2 tablespoons queso fresco and a sprinkle of onion on the lower third of a tortilla, roll, and place on a warm individual plate, 3 enchiladas per serving, or on a warmed serving platter large enough to accommodate enchiladas in a single layer.

* When the enchiladas are plated, cover with the remaining sauce.

* Garnish with queso fresco, onion, lettuce, and radishes.

Enchiladas de Santa Clara

Yields 12 enchiladas / Serves 4

In this folded version of enchiladas, the tortillas are fried after being dipped in an uncooked chile and egg sauce. As the egg cooks, it gives a rustic appearance to the enchilada, adding texture and interest to the finished dish.

INGREDIENTS

For the sauce:

* 4 ancho chiles (60 grams), cleaned, destemmed, deseeded, and dry roasted (see page 58)
* 1 clove garlic, peeled and coarsely chopped
* 2 large eggs, lightly beaten
* Kosher salt to taste

For the filling:

* $^1\!/_2$ pound (227 grams) queso fresco, cut into 12 slices about $^3\!/_{16}$ inch (4.7 mm) thick

For the assembly:

* 12 corn tortillas, preferably a few days old
* Lard or vegetable oil as needed for frying

For the garnish:

* 2 cups (240 grams) queso añejo or queso fresco, crumbled

DIRECTIONS

Start with the sauce:

* Place the prepared chiles in hot water and soak for 10–15 minutes, or until soft.

* Drain the chiles, discard the soaking liquid, and place the chiles in a blender along with the garlic.

* Add enough fresh water to process to a smooth, medium sauce consistency.

* Salt to taste (slightly overseasoning to allow for the addition of eggs).

* Strain the sauce into a large bowl.

* Add the beaten eggs and whisk to combine.

Assemble the enchiladas:

* Place foil on the stove and backsplash to facilitate cleanup.

* Add lard or oil to a depth of ¼ inch (6 mm) in a heavy skillet over medium heat. Heat to low frying temperature, about 300°F (150°C). (If it is too hot, the sauce will burn, see note.)

* Dip each tortilla in the sauce, making sure to heavily coat.

* Place the tortilla in oil and fry for a few seconds on each side. Using a wide spatula, carefully remove the tortilla and drain on paper towels.

* Place a slice of queso fresco on one half of the tortilla and fold in half. It should be hot enough to soften the cheese.

* Place, slightly overlapping, on a warm individual plate, 3 enchiladas per serving.

* It is not necessary to pour additional sauce over the enchiladas.

* Garnish with queso añejo or queso fresco.

Note: A tomato and lettuce salad sprinkled with lime juice, salt, and pepper is an excellent accompaniment to this dish.

Enchiladas Suizas

Yields 12 enchiladas / Serves 4–6

Enchiladas Suizas was invented in 1950 at Sanborn's in the historic Casa de Aulejos (House of Tiles) in Mexico City. Suizas, *or "Swiss," refers to the dairy in the recipe.*

INGREDIENTS:

For the sauce:
* 1 pound (454 grams) tomatillos, husks removed, cored
* 1–2 serrano chiles, destemmed
* $\frac{1}{2}$ medium white onion, peeled, coarsely chopped, and root end removed
* 3 cloves garlic, peeled
* $\frac{3}{4}$ bunch cilantro
* 1 tablespoon (15 ml) vegetable oil
* 1 cup (237 ml) crema Mexicana
* Kosher salt to taste

For the filling:
* 2 cups (260 grams) poached and shredded chicken (see page 70)

For the assembly:
* 12 white corn tortillas
* Vegetable oil as needed for softening tortillas
* 2 cups (240 grams) queso asadero or queso Chihuahua, grated

For the garnish:
* 1 cup (237 ml) crema Mexicana
* White onion, peeled and thinly sliced
* Cilantro leaves

DIRECTIONS

Start with the sauce:

* Place the tomatillos, chiles, onion, and garlic in a saucepan, cover with water, and bring to a boil.

* Reduce heat to a simmer and gently cook until the tomatillos change color but do not burst.

* Using a slotted spoon, transfer vegetables to a blender, reserving cooking liquid.

* Blend the vegetables until smooth, adding cooking liquid as needed to achieve a medium sauce consistency.

* Add cilantro and process for a few seconds more.

* In a saucepan over medium heat, place 1 tablespoon (15 ml) oil.

* When it is hot, add the sauce and cook for a few minutes until warmed through and slightly thickened.

* Reduce to a bare simmer and stir in crema Mexicana. Heat the sauce through, but do not let it boil.

* Remove from heat and season with salt to taste. Cover, set aside, and keep warm.

Assemble the enchiladas:

* Preheat the oven to 350°F (177°C).

* Pour oil to a depth of ½ inch (12 mm) in a heavy skillet over medium-high heat. Heat to low frying temperature, about 300°F (150°C).

* Place each tortilla in the oil and fry for a few seconds, just long enough to soften. Drain on paper towels.

* Fill the lower third of a tortilla with 2 tablespoons shredded chicken, roll, and place seam side down in an ovenproof baking dish large enough to accommodate the enchiladas in a single layer.

* Repeat with the remaining tortillas.

* Generously cover with the sauce, making sure the edges of the enchiladas are well covered.

* Sprinkle queso asadero or queso Chihuahua on top.

* Bake in a preheated oven until the enchiladas are heated through and the cheese is melted and brown in spots, about 15 minutes.

* Garnish with crema Mexicana, onion slices, and cilantro leaves.

Note: These enchiladas are intended to be flavorful but not spicy hot, so use chiles accordingly.

Enchiladas Suizas, La Fonda on Main

Yields 12 enchiladas / Serves 4–6

In La Fonda's version of this classic enchilada recipe, pepitas add a nutty flavor to the sauce, and the enchiladas are topped with Swiss cheese and garnished with a refreshing Romaine Lettuce Salad.

INGREDIENTS

For the sauce:
* 2 tablespoons (30 ml) vegetable oil
* ⅓ cup (47 grams) white onion, diced
* 2–3 serrano chiles, destemmed and chopped (see note)
* 2 cloves garlic, peeled
* ½ cup (65 grams) raw pepitas (pumpkin seeds)
* 1 pound (454 grams) tomatillos, husks removed, quartered
* 1 cup (237 ml) crema Mexicana
* 1½ tablespoons (14 grams) kosher salt, or to taste

For the filling:
* 2 chicken breasts (approximately 1 pound, 454 grams), poached and shredded (see page 70)

For the assembly:
* 12 corn tortillas
* Vegetable oil as needed for softening tortillas
* 2 cups (240 grams) Swiss cheese, shredded (or substitute asadero or Chihuahua)

For the garnish:
* Romaine Lettuce Salad (see page 83)

DIRECTIONS

Start with the sauce:

* Place the oil in a sauté pan over medium heat.

* Add the onion, serrano chiles, garlic, and pepitas.

* Cook, stirring occasionally, until onion is translucent, 3–5 minutes.

* Add the tomatillos and cook for an additional 10 minutes, or until soft.

* Add crema Mexicana and salt to taste.

* Bring to a simmer and remove from heat. Allow to cool for a few minutes.

* Place the ingredients in a blender and purée in batches to a smooth consistency.

* Taste and adjust the seasoning.

Assemble the enchiladas:

* Prepare the romaine lettuce salad and vinaigrette. Store separately in the refrigerator until needed.

* The shredded chicken for the filling should be warm and at hand.

* Pour oil to a depth of ½ inch (12 mm) in a heavy skillet over medium heat. Heat to low frying temperature, about 300°F (150°C).

* Place each tortilla in the oil and fry for a few seconds, just long enough to soften. Drain on paper towels.

* Place 2 tablespoons shredded chicken on a softened tortilla, roll, and place in an ovenproof baking dish large enough to accommodate the enchiladas in a single layer.

* Repeat with the remaining tortillas.

* Top with the tomatillo sauce and cheese.

* Place under a broiler until the cheese melts and the top browns in spots, about 5 minutes.

* Cover loosely with foil and let rest for a few minutes.

* Toss the romaine lettuce salad mixture with the vinaigrette and sprinkle lengthwise down the center of the casserole.

Note: For a milder flavor, serranos should be deseeded.

Enchiladas Enjococadas

Yields 12 enchiladas / Serves 4

Jocoque, which comes from Nahuatl for "something sour," is a tangy, strained yogurt product introduced to Mexico by Lebanese immigrants. Enjococada means "to be immersed in Jocoque."

INGREDIENTS

For the sauce:

* 2 cloves garlic, unpeeled
* 3 pasilla chiles, cleaned, destemmed, deseeded, and dry roasted (see page 58)
* 2 cups (480 grams) jocoque or whole milk yogurt
* Heavy cream as needed for thinning sauce
* Kosher salt to taste

For the filling:

* 1 cup (120 grams) queso añejo or queso fresco, crumbled
* 1 cup (140 grams) white onion, finely chopped

For the assembly:

* 12 corn tortillas
* Vegetable oil as needed for softening tortillas

For the garnish:

* ¼ cup (30 grams) queso añejo or queso fresco, crumbled

DIRECTIONS

Start with the sauce:

* Dry roast the garlic on an unoiled comal or iron griddle over medium-high heat. When the garlic has a few brown spots, remove, peel, and set aside.
* Place the prepared pasilla chiles in a bowl, cover with water, and soak for about 10 minutes.
* Drain the chiles, discard the soaking liquid, and place the chiles in a blender along with the garlic.
* Add the jocoque or yogurt and pulse until smooth, adding heavy cream as needed to attain a light sauce consistency.
* Strain through a medium-mesh strainer.
* Pour the mixture into a saucepan over medium-low heat.
* Gently cook, stirring occasionally, until sauce slightly thickens, 8–10 minutes. Do not allow the sauce to boil.
* Season with salt to taste. Cover, set aside, and keep warm.

Prepare the filling:

* Mix the queso and onion together and set aside.

Assemble the enchiladas:

* Preheat the oven to 300°F (150°C).
* Pour oil to a depth of ½ inch (12 mm) in a heavy skillet over medium-high heat. Heat to low frying temperature, about 300°F (150°C).
* Place each tortilla in the oil and fry for a few seconds, just long enough to soften. Drain on paper towels.
* Dip a softened tortilla in the warm sauce.
* Place 2 tablespoons cheese/onion mixture on the sauced tortilla, fold in half, and place, overlapping slightly, on an individual ovenproof plate, 3 enchiladas per serving.
* Cover with the sauce, making sure the edges of enchiladas are well covered.
* Repeat with the remaining tortillas.
* When the enchiladas are plated, garnish with queso añejo or queso fresco and place in a preheated oven just long enough to warm through.

Note: The enchiladas may also be rolled and placed in a casserole large enough to accommodate them in a single layer. Garnish and place in a preheated 300°F (150°C) oven just long enough to warm through.

Envueltos de Nata

Yields 12 enchiladas / Serves 6

Envueltos, *which means "to wrap," is a term used in the state of Puebla for enchiladas.* Nata *translates as the thick layer of cream that forms on the surface of cooked milk, which is very similar to English clotted cream or Serbian kaymak. Heavy cream is used here.*

INGREDIENTS

For the sauce:

* 1 pound (454 grams) Roma tomatoes
* ¹⁄₂ medium white onion, unpeeled
* 2 cloves garlic, unpeeled
* 8 poblano chiles, fire roasted, peeled, seeded, and deveined (see page 57), divided (¹⁄₄ for sauce, ³⁄₄ reserved for filling)
* 2 tablespoons (30 ml) vegetable oil
* 2 tablespoons (28 grams) unsalted butter
* 1 cup (237 ml) heavy cream
* Kosher salt to taste

For the filling:

* 2 cups (160 grams) panela cheese, grated
* Reserved poblano chiles

For the assembly:

* 12 corn tortillas
* Vegetable oil as needed for softening tortillas

For the garnish:

* Panela cheese, grated

DIRECTIONS

Start with the sauce:

* Dry roast the tomatoes, onion, and garlic on an unoiled comal or iron griddle set over medium-high heat (see page 59).

* After dry roasting, core the tomatoes, discard the papery outer layer of onion skin, and peel the garlic.

* Place the tomatoes, onion, and garlic in a blender. Process at medium speed until smooth. Set aside.

* Cut the prepared poblano chiles into strips.

* Heat the oil and butter in a saucepan over medium heat. Add the prepared poblano strips and sauté for 2 minutes. Remove three-quarters of the poblano strips from the pan, cover, and keep warm. (These will go in the filling.)

* Pour the tomato mixture into a saucepan with the remaining poblano strips. Sauté until the mixture slightly reduces and the color changes to a dark orange.

* Stir the cream into the tomato/poblano mixture and cook for 3–5 minutes, or until heated through. Do not boil. Season with salt to taste. Cover and keep warm.

Prepare the filling:

* Mix the panela cheese with the reserved poblano strips.

* Cover and keep warm.

Assemble the enchiladas:

* Pour oil to a depth of ½ inch (12 mm) in a heavy skillet over medium-high heat. Heat to low frying temperature, about 300°F (150°C).

* Place each tortilla in the oil and fry for a few seconds, just long enough to soften. Drain on paper towels.

* Dip each tortilla in the warm tomato/poblano/cream sauce. Place 2 tablespoons poblano/cheese mixture on the lower third of a tortilla, roll, and place on a warm individual plate, 2 per serving, or on a warm casserole large enough to accommodate the enchiladas in a single layer.

* Cover with the remaining sauce.

* Garnish with panela cheese.

Enchiladas Berenjenas * PAGE 192

Vegetable
Verdura

Poblano Cream Sauce

Yields 4 cups (1 liter)

This sauce is used with Enchiladas Berenjenas (see page 192) and Enchiladas Espinacas (see page 194).

INGREDIENTS

* 5 poblano chiles, fire roasted, peeled, deseeded, and deveined (see page 57)
* ½ medium yellow or white onion, peeled, medium dice
* 2 teaspoons (5 grams) garlic, minced
* 1½ cups (355 ml) half and half
* 1 tablespoon (9 grams) kosher salt
* Drizzle of vegetable oil
* 1 teaspoon (5 grams) unsalted butter

DIRECTIONS

* Roughly chop the prepared poblano chiles.
* Add the butter and a drizzle of oil to a saucepan over medium heat. Add the diced onion and sauté until translucent, 3–5 minutes.
* Add the garlic and sauté for 1 additional minute.
* Stir in the poblanos.
* Add the half and half and salt to the saucepan and stir to combine. Bring to a simmer and cook for about 2 minutes. Remove from heat and allow to cool for a few minutes.
* Pour into a blender and purée until smooth. (Be careful not to overfill blender; if necessary, process the sauce in batches.)
* If proceeding immediately with a recipe, return the sauce to the saucepan, cover, and keep warm, but do not boil.

Note: *Sauce may be refrigerated for up to 5 days.*

Chipotle Sauce

Yields 4 cups (1 liter)

This sauce is used with Enchiladas de Camarón (see page 154), Enchiladas de Camarón y Nopales (see page 156), Enchiladas Rojas de Queso (see page 174), Enchiladas de Camote (see page 198), and Enchiladas de Nopales (see page 208).

INGREDIENTS

* 2 ½ pounds (1.13 kilos) Roma tomatoes
* 2 tablespoons (30 ml) vegetable oil
* ½ medium yellow or white onion, peeled and chopped
* 1 ½ teaspoons (4 grams) garlic, minced
* 2 large chipotles en adobo, destemmed and minced
* Kosher salt to taste (about 1 tablespoon, 9 grams)

DIRECTIONS

* Preheat the oven to 350°F (177°C).
* Place the tomatoes in a single layer on a foil-lined baking sheet. Roast, turning occasionally, until the skins begin to burst and the tomatoes are soft, about 25 minutes
* Place under a broiler for about 5 minutes to blacken the skins in spots. Set aside to cool for a few minutes.
* Place the oil in a saucepan over medium heat.
* Add the onion and cook until translucent but not brown, 3–5 minutes.
* Add the garlic and chipotles en adobo and cook for 1 additional minute.
* Place the onion mixture and tomatoes in a blender and purée until smooth.
* Add salt to taste.
* Strain the sauce through a medium-mesh strainer.
* If proceeding immediately with an enchilada recipe, pour the sauce into a saucepan over medium-low heat, cover, and keep warm.

Note: *Sauce may be refrigerated for up to 5 days.*

Enchiladas Berenjenas (Eggplant)

Yields 12 enchiladas / Serves 4–6

Technically this is not a true enchilada, because the filling is wrapped with an eggplant slice instead of a corn tortilla, but the presentation, enrollada y enchilada *(rolled and sauced with chile), is similar to many enchilada recipes and a delicious vegetarian option. Corn tortillas still make it into the recipe—they are served on the side.*

INGREDIENTS

For the eggplant wrapping:
* 2 large purple eggplants, ends trimmed

For the sauce:
* 1 recipe Poblano Cream Sauce (see page 190)

For the filling:
* 1 cup (140 grams) zucchini, small dice
* 1 cup (140 grams) yellow squash, small dice
* 1 cup (140 grams) red onion, small dice
* 2–3 cups (240–360 grams) queso asadero, grated (some reserved for topping)
* 1 tablespoon (15 ml) vegetable oil
* Kosher salt to taste

For the garnish:
* Black Bean Relish (see page 82)
* Corn tortillas on the side

DIRECTIONS

Start with the eggplant wrapping:

* Cut the eggplants lengthwise into ⅛-inch (3 mm) slices (1 slice per enchilada). Brush lightly with oil and season with salt. Grill 30 seconds per side, or until slightly soft but not falling apart. Set aside.

Prepare the sauce:

* Prepare the poblano cream sauce as directed (see page 190).
* If the sauce was prepared ahead of time, reheat in a saucepan over medium-low heat. When heated, reduce heat to very low, cover, and keep warm, but do not allow to boil.

Make the filling:

* Place the oil in a sauté pan over medium heat. When the oil is hot, add the zucchini, yellow squash, onion, and a pinch of salt.
* Sauté the vegetables, stirring occasionally, until tender, about 5 minutes.
* Add 1 cup (120 grams) queso asadero. Toss together until the cheese is melted. Adjust the seasoning, set aside, and keep warm.

Assemble the enchiladas:

* Preheat the oven to 325°F (163°C).
* Have the garnishes ready and at hand.
* Place approximately 2 tablespoons filling on the lower third of an eggplant slice and roll up. Place in an ovenproof baking dish large enough to accommodate the enchiladas in a single layer.
* Repeat with the remaining eggplant slices.
* When the slices are filled and rolled, cover with the poblano cream sauce and 1–2 cups (120–240 grams) queso asadero. Place in the oven just long enough to melt the cheese.
* Garnish with the black bean relish just before serving.
* Serve warm corn tortillas on the side.

Enchiladas Espinacas (Spinach)

Yields 12 enchiladas / Serves 4

INGREDIENTS

For the sauce:

* 1 recipe Poblano Cream Sauce (see page 190), divided (1 cup, 237 ml, reserved for filling)

For the filling:

* 2 tablespoons (30 ml) vegetable oil
* 3 cups (225 grams) mushrooms, chopped
* ¾ cup (105 grams) onion, minced
* 1 ¾ cups (190 grams) sun-dried tomatoes, minced
* 1 large bag (9 ounces, 255 grams) fresh spinach, divided (some leaves reserved for garnish)
* Kosher salt to taste
* 1 cup (237 ml) poblano cream sauce

For the assembly:

* 12 corn tortillas
* Vegetable oil as needed for softening tortillas and frying spinach leaves

For the garnish:

* 1 cup (120 grams) queso asadero or white Monterey Jack, grated
* Deep-fried spinach leaves
* Sun-dried tomatoes, chopped

DIRECTIONS

Start with the sauce:

* Prepare the poblano cream sauce as directed (see page 190).

* If the sauce was prepared ahead of time, reheat in a saucepan over medium-low heat. When hot, reduce heat to very low, cover, and keep warm, but do not boil.

Prepare the filling:

* Place 2 tablespoons (30 ml) oil in a sauté pan over medium-high heat. When hot, add the mushrooms and sauté, tossing occasionally, until golden. Reduce heat to medium.

* Add the onion and sun-dried tomatoes and cook until the onion is translucent, 3–5 minutes. Add the spinach, generous handfuls at a time, adding more as it cooks down (reserve some leaves to fry for garnish). Sauté just until the spinach is wilted. Season with salt to taste. Drain any excess moisture from the pan.

Assemble the enchiladas:

* Preheat the oven to 325°F (163°C).

* Pour oil to a depth of ½ inch (12 mm) in a heavy skillet over medium-high heat. Heat to low frying temperature, about 300°F (150°C).

* Place each tortilla in the oil and fry for a few seconds, just long enough to soften. Drain on paper towels. Keep the oil hot for frying the spinach leaves.

* Fill the lower third of a softened tortilla with ¼ cup (60 grams) mushroom/spinach mixture and a drizzle of poblano cream sauce, roll, and place in an ovenproof dish large enough to accommodate the enchiladas in a single layer. (Enchiladas may also be served on individual ovenproof plates, 3 per serving.)

* Repeat with the remaining tortillas.

* Top the enchiladas with the remaining poblano cream sauce and sprinkle with queso asadero. Place in a preheated oven just long enough to melt the cheese.

* While the cheese is melting, scatter the reserved spinach leaves on the surface of the oil used for softening tortillas and fry just long enough to crisp. Remove with slotted spoon and drain on paper towels.

* Just before serving, garnish the enchiladas with the fried spinach leaves and bits of sun-dried tomato.

Enchiladas de Baja California

Yields 12 enchiladas / Serves 4

In this recipe, the tortillas are dipped in the sauce first and then fried. When adding salt to the sauce, don't be afraid to season aggressively—the salt moderates the heat of the serrano chiles.

INGREDIENTS

For the sauce:

* 3 ancho chiles (45 grams), cleaned, destemmed, deseeded, and dry roasted (see page 58)
* 3 whole black peppercorns
* 3–4 serrano chiles, dry roasted (see page 59)
* ¼ medium white onion, dry roasted
* 1 clove garlic, dry roasted
* 1 tablespoon (15 grams) lard or vegetable oil for frying
* Kosher salt to taste

For the filling:

* 2 cups (240 grams) queso asadero or panela cheese, grated
* 1 large Yukon Gold potato, peeled, medium dice, and simmered until tender, 6–8 minutes
* ¼ medium white onion, peeled and minced

For the assembly:

* 12 corn tortillas, preferably a few days old
* Vegetable oil as needed for frying

For the garnish:

* 1 cup (237 ml) crema Mexicana

DIRECTIONS

Start with the sauce:

* Cover the prepared ancho chiles with hot water and soak until softened, about 10 minutes. Drain and discard the soaking liquid.

* Place the softened chiles, peppercorns, and dry roasted serrano chiles, onion, and garlic in a blender.

* Add just enough water to process to a smooth purée.

* Heat 1 tablespoon (15 grams) lard or oil in a sauté pan over medium heat.

* Strain the sauce into the sauté pan and reduce heat to medium-low.

* Cook the sauce, stirring occasionally, until it darkens, 8–10 minutes. Add a little water as necessary to maintain a light sauce consistency.

* Add salt to taste.

* Cover, set aside, and keep warm.

Prepare the filling:

* Mix the cheese, potatoes, and onion together in a bowl.

Assemble the enchiladas:

* Place foil on the stove and backsplash to facilitate cleanup.

* Pour oil to a depth of ¼ inch (6 mm) in a heavy skillet or sauté pan over medium heat and bring to low frying temperature, about 300°F (150°C).

* Dip a tortilla in the sauce, allowing the excess to drain back into the pan.

* Place the sauced tortilla in the oil and fry for a few seconds on each side. (Be careful. If the oil is too hot, it will splatter.) Drain on paper towels.

* Place 2 tablespoons filling mixture on the bottom third of a tortilla, roll, and place on a warm individual plate, 3 per serving, or on a warmed serving platter large enough to accommodate the enchiladas in a single layer.

* Repeat with the remaining tortillas.

* When the enchiladas are plated, drizzle with crema Mexicana.

Note: *It is not necessary to top the enchiladas with additional sauce.*

Enchiladas de Camote (Sweet Potato)

Yields 12 enchiladas / Serves 4–6

INGREDIENTS

For the filling:

* 2 cups (460 grams, about 3 medium) sweet potatoes, roasted and mashed
* Kosher salt to taste

For the sauce:

* 1 recipe Chipotle Sauce (see page 191)

For the assembly:

* 12 tortillas
* Vegetable oil as needed for frying

For the garnish:

* Crema Mexicana
* Queso fresco
* 1 medium sweet potato, peeled and shredded for fried sweet potato strings or very thinly sliced lengthwise into chips (recipe follows)

DIRECTIONS

Start with the filling:

* Cut the tip off the narrow end of each sweet potato to keep it from bursting. Place on a foil-lined baking sheet in a 400°F (200°C) oven for about 1 hour, or until fork-tender. Cool for a few minutes.

* Once the sweet potatoes are cool enough to handle, peel and pass through a food mill or ricer to achieve a smooth consistency. Add salt to taste.

Prepare the sauce:

* While the potatoes are baking, prepare the chipotle sauce as directed (see page 191).

* If the sauce was prepared ahead of time, place it in a saucepan set over medium-low heat, cover, and keep warm.

Assemble the enchiladas:

* Preheat the oven to 140°F (60°C).

* In a deep skillet or Dutch oven, pour oil to a depth of 2 ½ inches (6.33 cm) and place over medium-high heat. Bring to medium frying temperature (about 350°F, 177°C).

* To soften the tortillas, wrap them in a clean kitchen towel, place in a plastic storage bag (do not seal), and microwave on high for 45–60 seconds.

* Place 2 tablespoons sweet potato purée on the lower third of a tortilla, roll, and skewer with a toothpick. Repeat with the remaining tortillas.

* Deep fry the enchiladas a few at a time (do not crowd) until crispy. Drain on paper towels and place on an ovenproof platter in the oven to keep warm. Continue frying the remaining enchiladas (allow the oil to reheat to frying temperature between batches).

* When ready to serve, remove the toothpicks, place 2–3 enchiladas per serving on warm individual plates, top with the chipotle sauce, and garnish with crema Mexicana, queso fresco, and (optional) fried sweet potato strings or slices.

SWEET POTATO CHIPS

How to make sweet potato strings or chips:

* Using a mandolin slicer, slice a peeled, raw sweet potato into very thin, long slices or shred into strings. Just before serving, place in a deep fryer at 350°F (177°C) until golden, drain on paper towels, and use as a garnish.

Enfrijoladas al Estilo de Oaxaca

Yields 12 enchiladas / Serves 4

Enfrijoladas are one of the most ancient, basic, and universally eaten enchiladas in Mexico. This version comes from the southwestern state of Oaxaca. A sprig of epazote, if available, is traditionally added to the bean pot and will enhance the flavor of the finished sauce.

INGREDIENTS

For the sauce:

* 3 Oaxacan pasilla chiles (or morita chiles), cleaned, destemmed, deseeded, and dry roasted (see page 58)
* 3 cups (720 grams) cooked black beans, plus bean cooking liquid as needed to thin the sauce (see page 60)
* 2 dried avocado leaves, if available (see page 17)
* 2 tablespoons (30 ml) vegetable oil (lard is traditional) for frying
* Kosher salt to taste

For the assembly:

* 12 corn tortillas
* Vegetable oil as needed for softening tortillas

For the garnish:

* Avocado slices
* 1/3 medium white onion, peeled and thinly sliced into rings
* 1/3 cup (40 grams) queso fresco, crumbled
* 3 parsley or cilantro sprigs

DIRECTIONS

Start with the sauce:

* Place the prepared chiles in hot water and soak for 10 minutes, or until soft. Drain and discard the soaking liquid.

* Place beans, avocado leaves (if available), chiles, and $^3/_4$ cup (178 ml) bean cooking liquid in a blender. Purée, adding a little more cooking liquid or water as needed to make a smooth, light sauce.

* Heat 2 tablespoons (30 ml) oil in a sauté pan over medium heat.

* Add the bean sauce and bring to a simmer. Season with salt to taste.

* Reduce heat to very low, cover, and keep warm. (Stir occasionally to keep a skin from forming on the surface. A little more bean cooking liquid or water may need to be added from time to time to maintain a light sauce consistency.)

Assemble the enchiladas:

* Pour oil to a depth of $^1/_2$ inch (12 mm) in a heavy skillet over medium-high heat. Heat to low frying temperature, about 300°F (150°C).

* Place each tortilla in oil and fry for a few seconds, just long enough to soften. Drain on paper towels.

* Dip each tortilla in the warm bean sauce, fold in half, and place on a warm individual plate, 3 enchiladas per serving.

* Top generously with more sauce.

* Garnish with avocado slices, onion, queso fresco, and parsley or cilantro sprigs.

Entomatadas with Chiles

Yields 12 enchiladas / Serves 4

This traditional tomato-sauced enchilada recipe from Oaxaca is usually served along with tasajo (salted and slightly dried beef), cecina enchilada (chile marinated and cooked pork), or pollo al oregano (chicken seasoned with garlic, oregano, and salt). The tortillas in Oaxaca are usually large (6 inches, 15 cm), so the entomatadas are folded into quarters. Smaller tortillas may be substituted and folded in half.

INGREDIENTS

For the sauce:

* 4–5 very ripe Roma tomatoes
* ½ small white onion, unpeeled
* 2 cloves garlic, unpeeled
* 1½–2 medium serrano chiles, or to taste
* 1½ tablespoons (22 ml) vegetable oil
* Kosher salt to taste

For the assembly:

* 12 corn tortillas
* Vegetable oil as needed for softening the tortillas

For the garnish:

* ⅓ cup (40 grams) queso fresco, crumbled
* Parsley or cilantro sprigs
* ½ small white onion, peeled and minced

DIRECTIONS

Start with the sauce:

* Dry roast the tomatoes, onion, garlic, and chiles on a comal or iron griddle over medium heat (see page 59).

* Peel the garlic. Trim the root end from the onion half, but do not peel. Remove the stem from serrano chiles, but do not deseed.

* Place the roasted vegetables and tomatoes in a blender. Process to a smooth purée, adding the serrano chiles to taste.

* Heat 1 1/2 tablespoons (22 ml) oil in a sauté pan over medium heat. Add the tomato sauce and fry, adding water as needed to attain a medium sauce consistency. Season with salt to taste. Cover, set aside, and keep warm.

Assemble the enchiladas:

* Pour oil to a depth of 1/2 inch (12 mm) in a heavy skillet over medium-high heat. Heat to low frying temperature, about 300°F (150°C).

* Place each tortilla in oil and fry for a few seconds, just long enough to soften. Drain on paper towels.

* Dip each tortilla in the sauce, fold in half, and place on a warm individual serving plate, 3 per serving.

* Top with additional sauce.

* Garnish with queso fresco, parsley or cilantro sprigs, and onion.

Note: *These enchiladas are traditionally served with meat on the side.*

Entomatadas without Chiles

Yields 12 enchiladas / Serves 4

Because of its mild flavor, this version is a particular favorite of small children.

INGREDIENTS

For the sauce:
* 1 pound (454 grams) Roma tomatoes
* 1 medium white onion, divided (½ reserved for garnish)
* 2 cloves garlic, peeled
* 2 tablespoons (30 ml) vegetable oil
* Kosher salt to taste

For the assembly:
* 12 corn tortillas
* Vegetable oil as needed for softening tortillas

For the garnish:
* ½ cup (60 grams) queso fresco, crumbled
* ½ reserved medium white onion, peeled and cut into thin, half-moon slices
* Parsley or cilantro sprigs

DIRECTIONS

Start with the sauce:

* Place the whole tomatoes in a saucepan.

* Add ¾ cup (178 ml) water, cover, and bring to a boil over medium-high heat. Cook until the skins of tomatoes are bursting, 2–3 minutes. Turn off heat, cover, and let the tomatoes cool in the pot.

* Cut the onion in half, pole to pole. Peel and coarsely chop one half. Peel other half and cut thin half-moon slices; reserve for garnish.

* Place the cooked tomatoes, coarsely chopped onion, and garlic in a blender and process until very smooth.

* Heat 2 tablespoons (30 ml) oil over medium-low heat and cook the sauce until the foam subsides and the flavors meld. Add salt to taste, cover, and keep warm.

Assemble the enchiladas:

* Have the garnishes ready and at hand.

* Pour oil to a depth of ½ inch (12 mm) in a heavy skillet over medium-high heat. Heat to low frying temperature, about 300°F (150°C).

* Place each tortilla in the oil and fry for a few seconds, just long enough to soften. Drain on paper towels.

* Pass the tortilla through the tomato sauce, fold in half, and place on a warm individual serving plate, 3 per serving.

* Cover with the remaining sauce.

* Garnish with queso fresco, onion slices, and parsley or cilantro sprigs.

Note: These enchiladas are traditionally served with meat on the side.

Enchiladas Mineras

Yields 12 enchiladas / Serves 4

The topping for these enchiladas is as important as the filling. For a firmer texture, napa cabbage may be substituted for the traditional iceberg lettuce.

INGREDIENTS

For the sauce:

* 8 guajillo chiles, cleaned, destemmed, deseeded, and dry roasted (see page 58)
* 2 cloves garlic, peeled
* ½ medium white onion, peeled and halved
* 1 teaspoon (2 grams) cumin seeds, toasted and ground
* 2 tablespoons (30 ml) vegetable oil for frying
* Kosher salt to taste

For the filling:

* 1 cup (120 grams) queso ranchero, grated (see note)
* ½ cup (70 grams) white onion, finely chopped
* Kosher salt to taste

For the assembly:

* 12 tortillas
* Vegetable oil as needed for frying

For the garnish:

* Shredded iceberg lettuce or napa cabbage
* 1 large carrot, peeled, medium dice, and simmered until tender, 6–8 minutes
* 1 medium Yukon Gold potato, peeled, medium dice, and simmered until tender, 6–8 minutes
* ½ cup (60 grams) queso ranchero, grated
* Jalapeños en escabeche (pickled), sliced

DIRECTIONS

Start with the sauce:

* Place the prepared guajillo chiles in a bowl and cover with boiling water. Soak for 10 minutes, or until soft.

* Drain and discard the soaking liquid. Place the chiles, garlic, onion, and cumin in a blender along with enough water to process, and purée until smooth. Strain through a medium-mesh strainer and set aside.

* Place 2 tablespoons (30 ml) oil in a large sauté pan over medium heat.

* When hot, add the strained sauce and cook, stirring occasionally, until slightly darker, about 15 minutes. If it is too thick, add a little water to attain a medium sauce consistency. Add salt to taste, cover, and set aside.

Prepare the filling:

* Mix queso ranchero with onion, add salt to taste, and set aside.

Assemble the enchiladas:

* Have the lettuce or cabbage, queso ranchero, and jalapeños en escabeche ready and at hand.

* Place foil on the stove and backsplash to facilitate cleanup.

* Pour ¼ inch (6 mm) oil into a heavy skillet over medium-high heat. Heat to medium frying temperature, about 350°F (177°C).

* Place the potatoes in the sauté pan and cook until they begin to brown. Add the carrots and sauté for an additional 2 minutes (for garnish).

* Remove the vegetables from pan, drain on paper towels, cover, and keep warm.

* Lower the temperature of the oil to 300°F (150°C).

* Dip a tortilla in sauce and fry for a few seconds on each side.

* Drain on paper towels.

* Stuff the bottom third of the tortilla with 2 tablespoons cheese/onion mixture.

* Roll and place on a warm individual plate, 3 per serving, or on a warmed serving platter large enough to accommodate the enchiladas in a single layer.

* Garnish with the lettuce or cabbage, carrots and potatoes, queso ranchero, and jalapeños en escabeche.

Note: Queso ranchero is a generic term for any fresh "ranch style" cheese. Queso fresco or queso blanco would work equally well.

Enchiladas de Nopales (Cactus)

Yields 12 enchiladas / Serves 6

These hearty but healthy enchiladas are filled with sautéed prickly pear cactus (nopales), Pico de Gallo, and scrambled eggs, topped with Chipotle Sauce, and garnished with queso fresco and Black Bean Relish.

INGREDIENTS

For the sauce:

* 1 recipe Chipotle Sauce (see page 191)

For the filling:

* ¼ cup (59 ml) vegetable oil
* 12 ounces (340 grams) nopales
* 1 ½ cups (355 ml) Pico de Gallo (see page 81)
* 6 large eggs

For the assembly:

* 12 red corn tortillas (or substitute yellow or white tortillas)
* Vegetable oil as needed for softening the tortillas
* Mexican White Rice (see page 66)

For the garnish:

* 1 ½ cups (180 grams) queso fresco, crumbled
* ¼ cup (59 ml) Black Bean Relish (see page 82)

DIRECTIONS

Start with the sauce:

* Prepare the chipotle sauce as directed (see page 191).

* If the sauce was prepared ahead of time, place in a saucepan over medium-low heat. When hot, reduce heat to low, cover, and keep warm.

Prepare the filling:

* Slice the nopales into ¼-inch (6 mm) strips. Rub well with kosher salt, rinse, and pat dry (see page 21).

* If using canned nopales, drain, rinse, and pat dry before proceeding.

* Place ¼ cup (59 ml) oil in a sauté pan over medium heat.

* When the oil is hot, add the prepared nopales (nopalitos) and pico de gallo, and sauté for 2 minutes.

* Just before assembly, reduce heat to low, add the eggs, and gently scramble with the other ingredients until the eggs are barely set and still moist. Remove from heat, cover, and keep warm.

Assemble the enchiladas:

* Pour oil to a depth of ½ inch (12 mm) in a heavy skillet over medium-high heat. Heat to low frying temperature, about 300°F (150°C).

* Place each tortilla in oil and fry for a few seconds, just long enough to soften. Drain on paper towels.

* For each serving, place ½ cup (80 grams) cooked white rice on a warm plate.

* Working quickly, place 2 tablespoons nopales mixture on the lower third of a tortilla, roll, and place on rice, 2 enchiladas per plate.

* Top with chipotle sauce and garnish with queso fresco and black bean relish.

Note: *Prepare the Pico de Gallo and Black Bean Relish first, to allow the flavors to meld.*

Enchiladas de Plátanos (Plantains)

Yields 12 enchiladas / Serves 6

In this recipe, the sweetness of plantains contrasts with the bright acidity of tomatillo and the spicy smokiness of chipotle, making these enchiladas an excellent accompaniment for grilled fish.

INGREDIENTS

For the sauce:

* 2 ancho chiles (30 grams), destemmed, deseeded, deveined, and dry roasted (see page 58)
* 2 pounds (907 grams) tomatillos, husks removed, cored
* 2 chipotles en adobo, stems removed
* 4 cloves garlic, dry roasted and peeled (see page 59)
* 2 tablespoons (30 ml) vegetable oil
* Kosher salt to taste

For the topping:

* 3 large, fully ripened (black) plantains, peeled and sliced into ½-inch (12 mm) diagonal pieces (36 slices total)
* ¼ cup (59 ml) vegetable oil for sautéing
* Kosher salt to taste
* ½ cup (60 grams) queso fresco or queso ranchero, crumbled

For the assembly:

* 12 corn tortillas
* Vegetable oil as needed for softening tortillas

For the garnish:

* Cilantro leaves (optional)
* ½ cup (118 ml) crema Mexicana

DIRECTIONS

Start with the sauce:

* Soak the prepared ancho chiles in hot water until tender, about 15 minutes. Drain and discard the soaking water.

* Place the tomatillos in a large pot of simmering salted water and cook until they change color, about 5 minutes.

* Remove the tomatillos from pot and place in a blender along with the ancho chiles, chipotles en adobo, and garlic and process until nearly smooth, being careful to maintain a little texture. Season with salt to taste.

* Heat 2 tablespoons (30 ml) oil in a saucepan and add the sauce.

* Cook, stirring occasionally, until the foam subsides and the sauce slightly darkens, about 10 minutes. Taste and adjust the seasoning. Cover, set aside, and keep warm.

Prepare the topping:

* Preheat the oven to 140°F (60°C).

* Cut plantains into ½-inch diagonal slices (about 36 slices will be needed).

* Heat ¼ cup (59 ml) oil in a large skillet over medium heat and fry about half the plantain slices (without overcrowding) until they are tender and golden brown on both sides, 6–8 minutes.

* Place on a cookie sheet lined with paper towels, lightly salt, and keep warm in a preheated oven while frying the remaining plantain slices.

Assemble the enchiladas:

* Add additional oil to the skillet to a depth of ½ inch (12 mm). Heat to low frying temperature, about 300°F (150°C).

* Place each tortilla in oil and fry for a few seconds, just long enough to soften. Drain on paper towels.

* Dip a softened tortilla in the sauce, making sure it is totally covered, fold in half, and place, slightly overlapping, on a warm individual plate, 2 per serving.

* Repeat with the remaining tortillas.

* When the enchiladas have been plated, top with queso fresco and fried plantain slices, about 6 per serving.

* Garnish with (optional) cilantro leaves and serve with crema Mexicana on the side.

Tex-Mex Beef Enchiladas * PAGE 216

Tex-Mex

Ancho Chile Gravy

Yields approximately 5 cups (1.2 liters)

Ancho chile gravy is used for Tex-Mex enchiladas. Fillings can be seasoned ground beef, shredded chicken, or grated longhorn cheddar cheese with minced white onion.

INGREDIENTS

For the ancho paste:

* 4 tablespoons (60 grams) ancho paste, made from 3 ancho chiles (see note)

For the ancho gravy:

* 8 tablespoons (113 grams) butter (or substitute lard or vegetable oil)
* 1 ½ teaspoons (3 grams) ground cumin
* 1 ½ teaspoons (4 grams) garlic, minced
* ½ cup (70 grams) all-purpose flour
* 4 cups (1 liter) chicken stock (see page 70)
* 4 tablespoons (28 grams) chile powder
* 4 tablespoons (60 grams) tomato paste
* Kosher salt to taste (approximately 1 tablespoon, 9 grams; less if using store-bought chicken stock)
* ¼ teaspoon (about 1 ml) apple cider vinegar, or to taste

DIRECTIONS

Start with the ancho paste:

* Remove the stems, seeds, and veins from the ancho chiles. Place in hot water to soak for approximately 15 minutes. Drain and discard the soaking liquid. Process the chiles in a blender with just enough fresh water to achieve a smooth paste. Four tablespoons (60 grams) will be needed for this recipe.

Prepare the gravy:

* Place butter, lard, or oil in a large sauté pan over medium heat. When hot, add the cumin and sauté for 1 minute. Add the garlic and sauté 1 additional minute.

* Add the flour and stir well. Cook over medium-high heat, stirring constantly, until the roux takes on a slightly golden color, 3–5 minutes.

* Place the chicken stock in a large saucepan and bring to a boil. Remove from heat and add the chile powder, 4 tablespoons (60 grams) ancho paste, tomato paste, 2 teaspoons (6 grams) salt, and apple cider vinegar. Mix thoroughly.

* When the roux is ready, add it slowly to the chicken stock mixture, stirring to combine.

* Place the gravy on medium-high heat and bring to a simmer, stirring constantly.

* When the gravy has thickened and is smooth, reduce heat to low and cook for 5 more minutes.

* Thin with a little chicken stock or water as needed to attain a medium gravy consistency. Add additional salt to taste.

Notes: *The paste from only about 1 $\frac{1}{2}$ ancho chiles is needed, but it is difficult to process fewer than 3 chiles in a blender. Process at least 3 ancho chiles and freeze the extra for other uses. (Three anchos will yield about 8 tablespoons chile paste.)*

Use ancho paste immediately, refrigerate for up to 1 week, or freeze for up to 1 month.

Store-bought chicken stock may be substituted, but reduce the amount of salt added to the recipe.

Tex-Mex Beef Enchiladas

Yields 12 enchiladas / Serves 4

The beef filling for this recipe is called a picadillo, *which can be translated as a "hash" or "mince" of meat and seasonings.*

INGREDIENTS

For the filling:

* 2 ½ pounds (1.13 kilos) ground beef
* 1 ½ cups (210 grams) yellow or white onion, small dice
* 1 ½ tablespoons (11 grams) garlic, minced
* 2 tablespoons (18 grams) kosher salt, or to taste
* 1 tablespoon (6 grams) ground cumin
* 1 tablespoon (6 grams) ground black pepper
* 2 bay leaves
* 2 serrano chiles, or to taste, minced
* 1 ½ cups (225 grams) Yukon Gold potatoes, peeled, small dice
* 1 ½ cups (225 grams) carrots, peeled, small dice
* 1 ½ cups (200 grams) Roma tomatoes, cored, deseeded, small dice

For the gravy:

* 4 cups (1 liter) Ancho Chile Gravy (see page 214)

For the assembly:

* 12 corn tortillas
* Vegetable oil as needed for softening tortillas

For the garnish:

* Colby or longhorn cheddar cheese, grated

DIRECTIONS

Start with the filling:

* Place the ground beef, ½ cup (118 ml) water, onion, garlic, salt, cumin, black pepper, and bay leaves in a large pot over medium heat.

* When the beef has begun to turn gray (about halfway cooked), break up and separate the meat with a heavy whisk or wooden spoon.

* Add the serrano chiles, potatoes, carrots, and tomatoes (in this order) and continue cooking, stirring occasionally to break up the meat and thoroughly mix the ingredients.

* When the meat begins to brown and the vegetables are tender, remove from heat. If not using picadillo immediately, cool, cover, and refrigerate until needed.

Assemble the enchiladas:

* Preheat the oven to 325°F (163°C).

* Warm the ancho chile gravy in a saucepan over low heat.

* Pour oil to a depth of ½ inch (12 mm) in a heavy skillet over medium-high heat. Heat to low frying temperature, about 300°F (150°C).

* Place each tortilla in oil and fry for a few seconds, just long enough to soften. Drain on paper towels.

* Spread 1 tablespoon gravy on a softened tortilla.

* Place 2 tablespoons picadillo on the lower third of a tortilla, roll, and place in a warm ovenproof casserole large enough to accommodate the enchiladas in a single layer.

* When the enchiladas have been plated, cover with the chile gravy, top generously with cheese, and bake in preheated oven until the enchiladas are heated through, 15–20 minutes.

Tex-Mex Cheese Enchiladas

Yields 12 enchiladas / Serves 4

The Tex-Mex cheese enchilada is a study in cultural fusion, coincidence, and availability of ingredients. The sauce, a chile gravy, evolved from the European tradition of thickening sauces with a roux and the coincidence that a German immigrant living in New Braunfels, Texas, William Gebhardt, began marketing Eagle Brand Chile Powder in the 1890s. This guaranteed year round availability of chiles and greatly simplified the preparation of any recipe that called for them. Cheddar cheese was probably chosen for the filling simply because it was the most commonly available cheese at the time.

Always use corn tortillas—red are traditional, but white or yellow tortillas may be substituted without any loss of flavor. Red corn tortillas originally got their color from ancho chile mixed into the masa, but today store-bought red tortillas are tinted with food coloring.

INGREDIENTS

For the gravy:

* 4 cups (1 liter) Ancho Chile Gravy (see page 214)

For the filling:

* 1 pound (454 grams) longhorn or Colby cheddar cheese, grated (some reserved for topping)
* 1 large white or yellow onion, peeled, small dice (optional)

For the assembly:

* 12 red corn tortillas (or substitute white or yellow tortillas, see note)
* Vegetable oil as needed for softening tortillas

DIRECTIONS

Assemble the enchiladas:

* Preheat the oven to 325°F (163°C).

* Warm the gravy in a saucepan over low heat. Add stock or water as needed to achieve a medium sauce consistency.

* Pour oil to a depth of ½ inch (12 mm) in a heavy skillet over medium-high heat. Heat to low frying temperature, about 300°F (150°C).

* Place each tortilla in oil and fry for a few seconds, just long enough to soften. Drain on paper towels.

* Spread a film of warm gravy on the bottom of a glass baking dish large enough to accommodate the enchiladas in a single layer.

* Spread 1 generous tablespoon gravy on a softened tortilla.

* Place 2 tablespoons cheese and a sprinkle of onion (optional) on the lower third of a tortilla, roll, and place in the baking dish.

* Repeat with the remaining tortillas.

* When the enchiladas have been rolled and plated, fully cover with the ancho chile gravy. Be careful to cover the edges of the tortillas.

* Top with the remaining cheese and (optional) onion and bake until the enchiladas are heated through, 15–20 minutes.

Note: *To make homemade red tortillas see page 53.*

Tex-Mex Chicken Enchiladas

Yields 12 enchiladas / Serves 4

INGREDIENTS

For the filling:

* 1½ pounds (680 grams) chicken leg quarters or thighs
* 1 pasilla chile, destemmed, deveined, deseeded, and dry roasted (see page 58)
* Kosher salt and ground black pepper to taste

For the gravy:

* 4 cups (1 liter) Ancho Chile Gravy (see page 214)

For the assembly:

* 12 corn tortillas
* Vegetable oil as needed for softening tortillas

For the garnish:

* Longhorn or Colby cheddar cheese, grated

DIRECTIONS

Start with the filling:

* Preheat the oven to 350°F (177°C).

* Place the chicken, skin side up, in a single layer on a sheet pan lined with aluminum foil.

* Place in the oven and bake until golden brown and fork-tender, about 1 hour.

* Remove from pan and, when cool enough to handle, discard the skin and bones (or save to make stock) and shred the meat into bite-size pieces.

* Place the pasilla chile in a coffee or spice grinder and process to a fine powder.

* Season the shredded chicken with salt, pepper, and ground pasilla chile to taste.

* If not using immediately, cover the chicken and refrigerate until needed.

Assemble the enchiladas:

* Preheat the oven to 325°F (163°C).

* Warm the gravy in a sauté pan over low heat. Add stock or water as needed to attain a medium sauce consistency.

* Gently reheat the shredded chicken, cover, and keep warm.

* Pour oil to a depth of ½ inch (12 mm) in a heavy skillet over medium-high heat. Heat to low frying temperature, about 300°F (150°C).

* Place each tortilla in the oil and fry for a few seconds, just long enough to soften. Drain on paper towels.

* Spread 1 generous tablespoon gravy on a softened tortilla.

* Place 2 tablespoons shredded chicken on the lower third of a tortilla, roll, and place on a warm individual plate, 3 per serving, or in a warm casserole large enough to accommodate the enchiladas in a single layer.

* When the enchiladas have been plated, cover with gravy, top with cheese, and bake in preheated oven until the enchiladas are heated through, 15–20 minutes.

Tex-Mex Brisket

Yields 4.8–6 pounds (2.2–2.7 kilos) cooked meat

INGREDIENTS

For the brisket:
* 1 (8–10 pound, 3.66–4.5 kilo) beef brisket, fat trimmed to ¼ inch (6 mm); 2 pounds needed for the enchiladas (see note)

For the wet rub mixture:
* 3 tablespoons (45 ml) vegetable oil
* 2 tablespoons (30 ml) whole grain mustard
* 2 tablespoons (14 grams) garlic, minced

For the dry rub mixture:
* 3 tablespoons (27 grams) kosher salt
* 3 tablespoons (40 grams) brown sugar
* 2 tablespoons (12 grams) whole black peppercorns, toasted and ground
* 1 teaspoon (2 grams) cumin seeds, toasted and ground
* 1 dried chile de árbol, ground
* 2 ancho chiles, ground

For the sauce part 1 (to be baked with brisket after it is smoked):
* 2 large white onions, peeled and diced
* 6 cloves garlic, peeled
* 3 bay leaves
* 1 small can jalapeños en escabeche (pickled), or to taste

For the sauce part 2 (added last 1 ½–2 hours of baking):
* 6 Roma tomatoes, cored
* 3 red jalapeños, destemmed, halved, and deseeded
* 3 cloves garlic, peeled

DIRECTIONS

Start with the brisket:

* Heavily apply the wet rub mixture followed by the dry rub mixture to the meat. Cover and refrigerate at least 2 days before proceeding.

* Bring the meat to room temperature 1 hour before placing it on a grill.

* Prepare the barbeque grill using a mixture of mesquite and oak charcoal. Allow the fire to burn down to 225–250°F (110–120°C). Push the coals to one side of the grill grate.

* When the fire is ready, place the brisket, fat side up, on the side of grill not directly over the coals.

* Cover and smoke the meat for 4 hours, maintaining a temperature of 225–250°F (110–120°C) and rotating the brisket 180 degrees once every hour for even cooking.

Add the sauce ingredients part 1 (to be baked with brisket after it has smoked):

* Toss together the onion, garlic, bay leaves, and jalapeños en escabeche with their liquid. Place in the bottom of an aluminum roasting pan large enough to accommodate the brisket.

* After the brisket has smoked for 4 hours, remove from the grill and place on top of the vegetables in the roasting pan.

Add the sauce ingredients part 2 (added last 1 ¹/₂ – 2 hours of baking):

* Cover the brisket tightly with aluminum foil and return to the grill, or place in oven, maintaining 225–250°F (110–120°C) temperature for 8 additional hours.

* For the last 1 ¹/₂–2 hours, add the tomatoes, red jalapeños, and additional garlic.

* After the cooking time is completed, remove the roasting pan from heat, uncover, and remove the brisket.

* If planning to make enchiladas, shred 2 pounds (907 grams) meat and return it to the pan to cool along with the vegetables and pan juices. (Reserve the remaining meat for other uses, see note.)

* When cool, remove the shredded meat from the pan and sprinkle with some pan juices.

* At this point, the meat may be covered and refrigerated for up to 5 days.

* Remove and discard the bay leaves. Remove and reserve the red jalapeños if making Tex-Mex Brisket Enchiladas (see page 224). Pour the pan juices and solids into a container, cover, and refrigerate for up to 5 days.

Note: *It is difficult to prepare less than an 8–10 pound (3.66–4.5 kilo) brisket and achieve good, moist results. Only approximately 2 pounds (907 grams) shredded brisket will be needed for the following enchilada recipe. Remainder may be served, sliced, as a main course, or used as a filling for tacos, chile rellenos, flautas, or tortas (sandwiches).*

Tex-Mex Brisket Enchiladas

Yields 12 enchiladas / Serves 4–6

INGREDIENTS

For the sauce:

* Pan juices and solids from a Tex-Mex smoked brisket (see page 222)
* Reserved red jalapeños from a Tex-Mex smoked brisket
* Kosher salt to taste

For the filling:

* 2 pounds (907 grams) cooked, shredded brisket
* 1 pound (454 grams) Oaxaca cheese, shredded (some reserved for topping)

For the assembly:

* 12 corn tortillas
* Vegetable oil as needed for softening tortillas

For the garnish:

* Avocado slices

Recommended accompaniment:

* Mexican White Rice (see page 66)

DIRECTIONS

Start with the sauce:

* Remove and discard the surface fat from the pan juices and solids before proceeding.
* Place the juices and solids in a saucepan and gently warm.
* Transfer the pan juices and solids to a blender. (Do not add red jalapeños yet.)
* Purée until smooth. Add salt to taste.
* With the blender running, add the red jalapeños, 1 at a time, until the desired level of heat is reached. Taste and adjust the seasoning as needed.
* Place the sauce in a saucepan over low heat. Cover and keep warm.

Assemble the enchiladas:

* Preheat the broiler.
* Place the shredded brisket in a saucepan, moisten with a little broth, and gently warm.
* Pour oil to a depth of $1/2$ inch (12 mm) in a heavy skillet over medium-high heat. Heat to low frying temperature, about 300°F (150°C).
* Place each tortilla in the oil and fry for a few seconds, just long enough to soften. Drain on paper towels.
* Spread 2 tablespoons sauce on a softened tortilla, followed by 2 tablespoons shredded brisket and a sprinkle of Oaxaca cheese.
* Roll and place the tortilla in a casserole dish large enough to accommodate the enchiladas in a single layer.
* Repeat with the remaining tortillas.
* When the enchiladas are plated, cover with the remaining sauce, top with the remaining Oaxaca cheese, and place under a preheated broiler until the cheese melts and browns in spots. Cover loosely with foil and let rest a few minutes.
* Garnish with avocado slices just before serving.
* Serve with Mexican white rice.

NOTES

Introduction

1 Michael Pollan, *The Omnivore's Dilemma: A Natural History of Four Meals*. New York: Penguin, 2006. 19.

2 P. J. White and L. A. Johnson, editors, *Corn: Chemistry and Technology*, 2nd ed. St. Paul, MN: American Association of Cereal Chemists, 2003. 3.

3 Michael Pollan, *The Omnivore's Dilemma: A Natural History of Four Meals*. New York: Penguin, 2006. 22.

4 Michael E. Smith, "City Size in Late Post-Classic Mesoamerica." *Journal of Urban History* 31, 4: 403–34. Estimates of the population of Tenochtitlán range as high as 300,000. At the time of the Conquest, the population was approximately four times the population of London.

5 Codex Mendoza, prepared on the order of Don Antonio de Mendoza, Viceroy of New Spain, for the Emperor Charles V, Mexico; c. 1535–50, Bodleian Library, MS. Arch. Selden. A. 1, fol. 60r.

6 John F. Mariani, *Encyclopedia of American Food and Drink*. New York: Lebhar-Friedman, 1999. 123.

7 Bernardino de Sahagún, *Historia general de las cosas de Nueva España*. 1558–1575. Chapter 19.

Ingredients: Chiles

1 Jan Timbrook, "The Natural History of Chile Peppers." Santa Barbara Museum of Natural History. www.sbnature.org/crc/332.html, September 4, 2013.

Ingredients: Nopales

1 Self NutritionData, nutritiondata.self.com/facts/vegetables-and-vegetable-products/3030/2. August 9, 2013.

Ingredients: Crema Mexicana

1 Diana Kennedy, *The Art of Mexican Cooking*, 2nd ed. New York: Clarkson Potter, 2008. 439.

Ingredients: Salt and Mexican Cuisine

1 Bernal Díaz del Castillo, *The Conquest of New Spain*. New York: Penguin Books. 150, 154.

Ingredients: Cilantro

1 Harold McGee. "Cilantro Haters, It's Not Your Fault." *New York Times*. www.nytimes.com/2010/04/14/dining/14curious.html. April 13, 2010.

Ingredients: Lard versus Vegetable Oil

1 Mayo Clinic Staff. "Transfat Is Double Trouble for Your Heart Health." www.mayoclinic.org/diseases-conditions/high-blood-cholesterol/in-depth/trans-fat/art-20046114. August 6, 2014.

RECIPE SOURCES

Most of the recipes in this book are traditional recipes without specific author attribution and are derived from numerous sources. However, we would like to acknowledge the following contributors.

Ancho Chile Gravy *
La Fonda on Main, San Antonio, Texas

Enchiladas de Atún *
Traditional recipe adapted by Chris Dunn, suggested by William Gonzalez

Enchiladas Banderas *
Traditional recipe adapted by La Fonda on Main, San Antonio, Texas

Enchiladas de Barbacoa *
Traditional recipe adapted by Chef Victor H. Maldonado, La Fonda on Main, San Antonio, Texas

Enchiladas Berenjenas *
La Fonda on Main, San Antonio, Texas

Black Bean Relish *
La Fonda on Main, San Antonio, Texas

Enchiladas Callejeras *
Traditional recipe adapted by Chef Victor H. Maldonado, La Fonda on Main, San Antonio, Texas

Enchiladas de Camarón *
Traditional recipe adapted by La Fonda on Main, San Antonio, Texas

Enchiladas de Camarón y Nopales *
Traditional recipe adapted by La Fonda on Main, San Antonio, Texas

Enchiladas de Camote *
Traditional recipe adapted by La Fonda on Main, San Antonio, Texas

Cebolla Encurtida *
Traditional recipe adapted by La Fonda on Main, San Antonio, Texas

Chipotle Sauce *
La Fonda on Main, San Antonio, Texas

Chorizo *
Chef Victor H. Maldonado, La Fonda on Main, San Antonio, Texas

Colored Tortillas *
La Fonda on Main, San Antonio, Texas

Enchiladas Divorciadas *
Traditional recipe adapted by La Fonda on Main, San Antonio, Texas

Enchiladas Enchorizadas *
Traditional recipe adapted by La Fonda on Main, San Antonio, Texas

Enfrijoladas al Estilo Oaxaca *
Traditional recipe adapted by Chef Iliana de la Vega, El Naranjo, Austin, Texas

Entomatadas with Chiles and without Chiles *
Traditional recipes adapted by Chef Iliana de la Vega, El Naranjo, Austin, Texas

Enchiladas Espinacas *
La Fonda on Main, San Antonio, Texas

Enchiladas de Frijoles y Chorizo *
Traditional recipe adapted by La Fonda on Main, San Antonio, Texas

Homemade Queso Fresco *
Luis Morales, Humble House Foods

Enchiladas Huastecas con Huevos *
Traditional recipe adapted by Chef Victor H. Maldonado, La Fonda on Main, San Antonio, Texas

Enchiladas de Langosta *
Chef Gabriel Ibarra, Cappy's Restaurant, San Antonio, Texas

Enchiladas de Machaca *
Traditional recipe adapted by La Fonda on Main, San Antonio, Texas

Mexican Rice Recipes *
La Fonda on Main, San Antonio, Texas

Enchiladas de Mole Rojo *
Traditional recipe adapted by Chef Iliana de la Vega, El Naranjo, Austin, Texas

Enchiladas Motuleñas *
Chef Victor H. Maldonado, La Fonda on Main, San Antonio, Texas, and
Chef Gabriel Ibarra, Cappy's Restaurant, San Antonio, Texas

Napa Slaw *
La Fonda on Main, San Antonio, Texas

Enchiladas de Nayarit *
Traditional recipe adapted by Chef Bianca Dorantes Valero

Enchiladas de Nopales *
Traditional recipe adapted by La Fonda on Main, San Antonio, Texas

Nopalito Salad *
La Fonda on Main, San Antonio, Texas

Enchiladas Norteñas *
Traditional recipe adapted by La Fonda on Main, San Antonio, Texas

Open-Faced Shrimp Enchiladas *
Chef Gabriel Ibarra, Cappy's Restaurant, San Antonio, Texas

Papadzules *
Traditional recipe adapted by Chef Iliana de la Vega, El Naranjo, Austin, Texas

Pastel Azteca *
Traditional recipe adapted by Chef Iliana de la Vega, El Naranjo, Austin, Texas

Enchiladas de Pato *
Traditional recipe adapted by La Fonda on Main, San Antonio, Texas

Pico de Gallo *
Traditional recipe adapted by La Fonda on Main, San Antonio, Texas

Pipián and Pork Enchiladas *
Traditional recipe adapted by La Fonda on Main, San Antonio, Texas

Enchiladas Placeras *
Inspired by a traditional recipe in *The Art of Mexican Cooking*, by Diana Kennedy

Enchiladas de Plátanos *
Adapted from a recipe in *A Cook's Tour of Mexico: Authentic Recipes from the Country's Best Open-Air Markets, City Fondas, and Home Kitchens*, by Nancy Zaslavsky

Enchiladas de Playa *
La Fonda on Main, San Antonio, Texas

Poblano Cream Sauce *
La Fonda on Main, San Antonio, Texas

Roasted Tomato Salsa *
Traditional recipe adapted by La Fonda on Main, San Antonio, Texas

Enchiladas Rojas *
Adapted from a recipe in *Mexico the Beautiful*, by Marilyn Tausend

Enchiladas Rojas de Queso *
Traditional recipe adapted by La Fonda on Main, San Antonio, Texas

Romaine Lettuce Salad *
La Fonda on Main, San Antonio, Texas

Enchiladas de Ropa Vieja *
Traditional recipe adapted by La Fonda on Main, San Antonio, Texas

Enchiladas de Santa Clara *
Inspired by a traditional recipe in *The Art of Mexican Cooking*, by Diana Kennedy
Recipe source: Hortensia Fagoaga

Salsa Cruda *

Traditional recipe adapted by La Fonda on Main, San Antonio, Texas

Enchiladas del Suelo *

Adapted from a recipe by Chef Alma Cervantes presented at the 2011
Culinary Institute of America Latin Flavors, American Kitchens Symposium

Enchiladas Suizas *

Traditional recipe adapted by Chef Iliana de la Vega, El Naranjo, Austin, Texas
Original recipe from Sanborn's, Casa de Aulejos, Mexico City

Enchiladas Suizas, La Fonda on Main *

Traditional recipe adapted by Chef Victor H. Maldonado, La Fonda on Main, San Antonio, Texas

Tex-Mex Beef Enchiladas *

Traditional recipe adapted by La Fonda on Main, San Antonio, Texas

Tex-Mex Cheese Enchiladas *

Traditional recipe adapted by La Fonda on Main, San Antonio, Texas

Tex-Mex Chicken Enchiladas *

Traditional recipe adapted by La Fonda on Main, San Antonio, Texas

Tex-Mex Brisket and Brisket Enchiladas *

Ceasar Zepeda, La Fonda on Main, San Antonio, Texas

Enchiladas Verdes de Pollo *

Traditional recipe adapted by La Fonda on Main, San Antonio, Texas

GLOSSARY OF SPANISH TERMS

achiote: Annatto seed. Adds a deep orange-red color and slightly nutty, peppery flavor to dishes.

adobo: In Mexico, a sauce with tomatoes, garlic, vinegar, spices, and salt. *Chipotles en adobo* are smoked jalapeño chiles en adobo sauce.

aguacate: Avocado.

al estilo de: In the style of. A reference to food prepared in a manner that is typical of a particular place, such as *al estilo de Oaxaca* (Oaxacan style).

arroz: Rice. Comes from the Arabic word *al rruz*.

atún: Tuna.

banderas: Flags. A trio of enchiladas that resembles the colors of the Mexican flag.

barbacoa: Traditionally, a cow's head (sometimes goat, lamb, or pork) that is baked in a pit covered with agave leaves or slow smoked over a fire.

berenjenas: Eggplant.

callejeras: Street style.

camarón/camarones: Shrimp.

camote: Sweet potato.

canela: Mexican cinnamon, which is true cinnamon from Sri Lanka.

carne de cerdo: Pork.

carne de res: Beef.

cascabel: Rattle or jingle bell. A name for both a small, ball shaped chile and, in the north central part of Mexico, the guajillo chile. The name refers to the sound the seeds make when the dried chile is shaken.

cebolla encurtida: Pickled onion.

cecina: Thinly sliced, salted, and air dried beef.

chiltomate: A spicy chile-tomato sauce that originated in the Yucatán.

chorizo: In Mexico, a fresh pork sausage seasoned with achiote and Mexican oregano.

cilantro: Leafy parts of the coriander plant.

comal: Flat griddle used for cooking tortillas and dry roasting chiles and vegetables.

comino: Cumin seed. *Comino molido* is ground cumin.

conquista: The conquest of Mexico by Spain, 1519–1521.

crema Mexicana: Mexican version of sour cream similar to crème fraiche.

del suelo: Of the soil. Sinaloa style enchilada.

deshebrada: Shredded. Cooked pork, beef, or chicken that is torn into bite-size pieces for use in Mexican cuisine.

divorciadas: Two enchiladas with contrasting sauces served side by side.

enchorizadas: Enchiladas topped with chorizo sauce.

encurtida: Pickled (*see* cebolla encurtida).

enfrijoladas: Enchiladas topped with bean sauce.

enjococadas: Enchiladas topped with jocoque (*see* jocoque).

enmoladas: Enchiladas topped with mole (*see* mole).

entomatadas: Enchiladas topped with tomato sauce.

envueltos: Wrapped. A term used in the state of Puebla for enchiladas.

epazote: A culinary and medicinal herb with a pungent aroma and flavor.

escabeche: Fish, meat, vegetables, or chiles marinated in an acidic mixture.

fajitas: Grilled beef skirt steak served with tortillas and condiments. May also refer to grilled chicken and shrimp served in a similar way.

flauta: Flute. A tortilla rolled around a filling and deep-fried.

frijoles: Beans.

frijoles negros: Black beans.

guarniciones: Accompaniments.

hoja santa: A large-leafed aromatic herb native to southern Mexico.

huitlacoche: A fungus that grows on corn that is highly prized for its earthy flavor.

jaiba: Blue crab.

jitomate: An alternate name for *tomate* (tomato) in some areas of Mexico.

jocoque: From the Nahuatl word for "something sour," a tangy, strained yogurt product introduced to Mexico by Lebanese immigrants.

lactéos: Dairy.

langosta: Lobster.

machaca/machacado: From *machacar*, which means "to pound." Cooked, dried, and pounded beef.

maguey: A type of agave used for making tequila, mescal, pulque, and agave nectar. The fibers are also used for rope and cloth, and in culinary applications.

maíz: Corn.

mariscos: Seafood.

masa: Dough made from freshly ground nixtamalized corn.

Mexican oregano: Various herbs that have an oregano-like flavor.

molcajete: Three-legged basalt mortar used to grind ingredients in Mexican cuisine. The pestle is called a *tejolote*.

mole: From the Nahuatl *mōlli*, for "sauce." Various sauces based on chiles and additional ingredients ranging from herbs and spices to nuts, seeds, and fruit.

Moros y Cristianos: "Moors and Christians," refers to a dish made of rice and black beans. The name has its roots in Spanish history when the Moors conquered and occupied Spain.

Nahuatl: An Uto-Aztecan language still spoken in parts of Mexico today. English words of Nahuatl origin include "avocado," "chili," "chocolate," and "tomato."

nata: The thick layer of cream that forms on the surface of cooked milk, similar to clotted cream.

nixtamalization: The process of soaking corn in a heated alkaline solution of slaked lime (calcium hydroxide) to improve the flavor and nutritional content of the grain.

nopales: Cactus paddles. *Nopalitos* are sliced cactus paddles.

norteñas: Northern style, often featuring beef.

papadzules: Possibly a pre-Columbian enchilada with hard cooked egg filling and topped with a pumpkin seed sauce and a tomato/habanero sauce.

pastel: Cake. Pastel Azteca is a layered casserole.

pato: Duck.

pepitas: Hulled pumpkin seeds.

picadillo: A hash or mince of meat and seasonings.

pico de gallo: "Rooster's beak." A generic term for various fresh salsas that usually contain a combination of chopped tomatoes, onion, cilantro, fresh hot chiles, lime juice, and salt. Sometimes fruit, cucumbers, and other ingredients are incorporated.

pipián: A type of mole that features squash seeds and chiles.

plátanos: Plantains.

playa: Beach. Enchiladas featuring seafood.

pollo: Chicken.

pulque: A milky-colored, slightly sour and yeasty tasting alcoholic beverage made from the fermented sap of maguey (agave) plants.

queso: Cheese.

rajas: Strips or cuts, often used in reference to sliced poblano chiles.

ranchero: Ranch style.

regias: Regal.

relleno: Filled. Often used to describe a poblano chile that has been stuffed with meat, cheese, and/or vegetables.

rojo: Red.

ropa vieja: Old clothes. Refers to meat that has the ragged appearance of old clothes.

salsa: Sauce. In Mexico, salsa refers to both cooked and raw sauces. In the United States, it most often refers to fresh, raw salsas, such as pico de gallo.

salsa cruda: A raw or uncooked sauce. In this book, it refers to a salsa made of puréed tomatillos and avocados.

suizas: Swiss style enchiladas, indicating the large amount of dairy in the recipe.

tapatias: Enchiladas in the style associated with the city of Guadalajara. A Tapatío is someone from Guadalajara.

teosinte: Wild grasses native to Central Mexico and ancestors of modern corn.

torta: Sandwich.

verde: Green.

Our Story

Growing up in San Antonio in the '50s and '60s, I thought I knew all about enchiladas. Our school cafeterias at Alamo Heights served them without fail every Wednesday. Most cafés in South Texas served enchiladas, rice, and beans, and the deluxe plate added a crispy taco. Everyone knew enchiladas were corn tortillas dipped in hot oil to soften and flavor, filled with yellow cheese and rolled into flutes. Then they were smothered with a tomato chili gravy, topped with more of the same cheese, and melted in a hot oven. To me, enchiladas were all pretty similar—they tasted good when they were hot and I was hungry; however, a half hour later I felt sleepy and stuffed.

In my late teens, I remember having green enchiladas for the first time. Gourmet stuff. Same rolled corn tortillas but filled with tender chicken topped with a tart green sauce made with an unripened tomato-looking fruit/vegetable that came in a husk called a *tomatillo*. Instead of yellow cheese, these green enchiladas had melted white cheese and a dollop of sour cream. Definitely different, decidedly delicious. While they were still called enchiladas and defined as Mexican food, they seemed lighter and more flavorful.

On my first visit to Mexico in my early 20s, I ate in restaurants and private homes and from street vendors. It was a revelation. The masa for the tortillas was made fresh each morning; the tortillas were wonderful and didn't need butter. The beans were black, savory and flavored with herbs I had never tasted. There was no yellow cheese, but it was the best cheese I had ever had. There was no gravy—just delicious sauces and salsas and a plethora of them. The cooks (*cocineros/as*) were proud, kind, and a bit secretive. That trip opened my eyes to a new view of Mexico and her amazing foods, particularly enchiladas of all colors, flavors, and design. I learned that enchiladas are the everyday food of Mexicans and vary greatly by region and cook. Perhaps even Hernán Cortés would agree—enchiladas are the true *tesoros de México*.

In later years, my wife Suzy and I took numerous trips throughout Mexico. We're still enthralled with the food markets, the variety of foods, and the warmth of the Mexican people. We have visited countless kitchens and have met talented chefs and even more amazing cooks. Mexico is a geographically diverse and breathtaking country with a big heart. Each region of this vast country has its own favorite dishes and especially its own enchiladas. Wild mushrooms from the mountains above Oaxaca; freshly caught shrimp in Mazatlán; pumpkin blossoms in Cuernavaca; and hand-crafted cheeses—all are creatively developed into memorable fillings for enchiladas.

Now in my 60s, I have made food and restaurants my primary career, conceiving, designing, and developing concepts and restaurants throughout Texas, some 29 altogether; however, never a Mexican restaurant until 1997. It was then that Suzy and I bought and rebuilt the oldest continuously operating Mexican restaurant in San Antonio, La Fonda on Main. In 1932, an industrious woman named Virginia Berry and her family opened this famous and historic venue. For years this acclaimed restaurant had served the city and its most famous visitors. The list of presidents, generals, movie stars, and other celebrities served at La Fonda on Main is long, and its dining awards were many. When we stepped in, the restaurant was 65 years old, tired, and worn out. The menu was limited and solely Tex-Mex.

By 1997, San Antonio was nationally famous for Tex-Mex cuisine, but few people knew of the more complex flavors of the whole of Mexico. There were already hundreds of "Mexican" restaurants and cafés. We had a major challenge: to restore a well-loved institution without losing generations of guests and to move the food forward without alarming longtime supporters. We kept the best of the Tex-Mex menu items and began introducing less-familiar dishes from interior Mexico. The first several years were tough going. Many old timers protested our menu redesign. Some questioned why we would have seafood on a Mexican menu and asked, "What in the world is *mole*?" and "What are *nopalitos*?" Finally, after several years, we managed to convince many that the flavors of Mexico are delicious, memorable, and great reasons to come back for more.

One thing we've learned as we've developed our menu and blackboard specials: people are willing to try almost anything described as an enchilada. The recipes in this book are by no means all the enchiladas of Mexico, Central America, and the southern United States. They are favorites from our restaurant that we have developed from many sources and that have passed the "guest test." Today, La Fonda on Main is again a very successful restaurant, serving more than 500 patrons daily. It has been a rewarding privilege to restore this legendary landmark and now to share our discoveries with you.

Our Team

Since purchasing La Fonda on Main, one of our biggest challenges has been a team that understands and shares our vision of a true Mexican restaurant. The staff at La Fonda on Main is made up of an extraordinary and committed group of caring professionals. Our General Manager, Ceasar Zepeda, was brought up in South Texas and weaned on Tex-Mex. Victor Maldonado, our Executive Chef, is from Huihitla, Mexico, and learned from his grandmother and mother in their famous home-restaurant known for serving authentic dishes from all over Mexico. Ceasar and Victor have worked hard to deliver and create menus at La Fonda on Main from their personal experience and knowledge of the best of interior Mexican and Tex-Mex cuisine.

After many years and innumerable requests, we finally found the time and resources to make this book a reality. Our good friend and food writer Chris Waters Dunn has done an extraordinary job of thoroughly researching the origins of the enchilada, including the history of corn, masa, and tortillas. He gathered recipes and perfected procedures. Our group spent hours discussing our collective love of Mexico and enchiladas of all shapes, sizes, flavors, and origins from virtually every region of Mexico, and Chris painstakingly converted this passion into a definitive and informative book on enchiladas.

Many have contributed to the brainstorming sessions, recipe development, tastings, food styling, and photo shoots. Trevor Lawton, our son and General Manager/Partner at Cappy's Restaurant, spent summers in Cuernavaca learning Mexican culture and the Spanish language. Trevor has a great palate and sincere interest in the food of Mexico. Gabriel Ibarra, Executive Chef at Cappy's, is a true artist in the kitchen and one of our country's best chefs. Iliana de la Vega, former Culinary Institute of America instructor and owner of El Naranjo in Austin (formerly of Oaxaca, Mexico), is a nationally acclaimed expert on Mexican cuisine. Culinary Institute of America graduates Blyth Treuhaft and Bianca Dorantes Valero were a tremendous help in testing recipes. Regina Rocha, Special Events Manager at La Fonda on Main, grew up in Mexico City, Cocoyoc, and San Antonio. Sunni Hammer is a top photography graduate of the Savannah College of Art and Design. Mark Menjivar is an accomplished artist and photographer based in San Antonio. Chica Younger and Alicia Mendez generously provided some of the serving pieces used in the photos. Without the gifted art direction and dogged discipline of Andréa Caillouet, this group of cats would have remained unherded.

All deserve thanks and recognition for their efforts and contributions. We are very proud to work with such a talented and committed team of friends.

—Cappy Lawton

✣ ✣

✣ ✣

Front row (left to right): Trevor Lawton, Suzy Lawton, Cappy Lawton, Iliana de la Vega
Back row (left to right): Regina Rocha, Andréa Caillouet, Chris Waters Dunn, Gabriel Ibarra, Ceasar Zepeda, Victor Maldonado

RECIPE INDEX